WORKPLACE
WELLNESS

Quarto

© 2024 Quarto Publishing Group USA Inc.

This edition published in 2024 by Chartwell Books,
an imprint of The Quarto Group
142 West 36th Street, 4th Floor
New York, NY 10018 USA
T (212) 779-4972 F (212) 779-6058
www.Quarto.com

10 9 8 7 6 5 4 3 2 1

Chartwell titles are also available at discount for retail, wholesale, promotional, and bulk purchase. For details, contact the Special Sales Manager by email at specialsales@quarto.com or by mail at The Quarto Group, Attn: Special Sales Manager, 100 Cummings Center Suite 265D, Beverly, MA 01915, USA.

ISBN: 978-0-7858-4474-7

Publisher: Wendy Friedman
Publishing Director: Meredith Mennitt
Editor: Jennifer Kushnier
Designer: Sue Boylan

All stock photos and design elements ©Shutterstock

Printed in China

This book provides general information. It should not be relied upon as recommending or promoting any specific diagnosis, method of treatment for a particular condition, or for promoting or recommending career advice. It is not intended as a substitute for medical advice or for direct diagnosis and treatment of a medical or psychological condition by a qualified physician or therapist. Readers who have questions about their career, or a particular condition, possible treatments for that condition, or possible reactions from the condition or its treatment should consult a career counselor, or physician, therapist, or other qualified healthcare professionals.

WORKPLACE
WELLNESS

A GUIDED WORKBOOK
FOR WHEN YOUR JOB IS DRIVING YOU CRAZY

SUSAN REYNOLDS

chartwell
books

Contents

Introduction

There's likely no place in your life that generates more stress than your workplace. Demanding bosses (or workloads), unrealistic expectations and deadlines, the necessity to constantly monitor and respect coworkers' needs, and the sheer length of time spent in your workplace all wear you down. Unfortunately, many of us are also standing for hours, doing repetitive work on assembly lines, or hyper-focused on a project that requires physical endurance; or we're "chained" to our desks, spending hours on our computers, fielding phone calls, congruently working on multiple projects, or succumbing to distractions (and thereby increasing stress levels). And in many workplaces, one has to deal with less-than-ideal conditions, heavy workloads, problematic coworkers, and demanding supervisors. No wonder it upsets your health!

WHY WORKPLACE WELLNESS MATTERS

While many workplaces now offer workplace wellness programs, it's typically up to the employee to take advantage of them—and it's far more common that the employee is *solely* responsible for his or her own workplace wellness.

Bolstering wellness in the workplace will make you happier while at work. Consider:

- Employees who take care of themselves find it easier to take the focus off their struggles and thus have greater ability to concentrate on their work.

- Healthy employees don't get sick as often.

- Well-cared-for employees are less likely to feel stressed, sleep deprived, or burned out and thereby have plenty of energy at work; they also have fewer workplace accidents.

- Employees who experience workplace well-being tend to be happier, have higher morale, and stay in their jobs longer.

Conversely, employees who don't practice workplace wellness often:

- Feel sleep deprived, due to long hours of work or worrying about work.
- Feel elevated levels of stress and anxiety both at work and at home.
- Don't have time or space for a social life.
- Are unable to break unhealthy habits such as smoking.
- Have difficulty creating healthy habits at work and at home.
- Experience more creative blocks.
- Have depleted energy levels and difficulty focusing.
- Suffer from disinterest or lack of motivation in the workplace.

Clearly, there are benefits to practicing workplace wellness; you don't need a book to tell you that. But wellness *can* seem overwhelming, especially if you don't feel supported on the job. Luckily, workplace wellness can be broken down into four aspects that *you* can improve—and that's where this book comes in.

FOUR ASPECTS OF WORKPLACE WELLNESS

The first step toward achieving wellness in the workplace is to take a realistic assessment of your work environment, on four primary levels:

Physical Environment

This is how your work *physically affects* your well-being. Does the environment protect and nurture your physical person? Do you feel safe commuting to, being at, and leaving work? Is the building well maintained? Is your workspace ergonomically protective? Is your workload too physically demanding? Are elements in your work environment negatively impacting your physical health? Ways to protect and improve your
physical wellness will be covered in Part I.

Emotional Challenges

This is how you *feel* while at work, or because of the work you do. Do you feel seen, heard, valued, sufficiently rewarded? Do you feel challenged, frustrated, overworked, underappreciated, unnecessarily stressed? Is it having an overall positive effect, or are you perpetually unhappy or frustrated? Any positive emotions generated by this specific job or workplace need to be noticed and reinforced; any negative ones need to be explored and challenged. Ways to protect and improve your emotional wellness will be covered in Part II.

Intellectual Fulfillment

This has to do with whether the work you do each day *challenges* you and *nourishes* who you are. Are you working above or below your intellectual capabilities? Do you often feel inadequate to successfully complete the tasks you are asked to do, or are you frequently bored at work? Is what you do each day in alignment with your values and goals? Does your company have a meaningful mission? Are you given opportunities for advancement? Ways to protect and improve your intellectual wellness will be covered in Part III.

> # "Never allow a person to tell you 'no' who doesn't have the power to say 'yes.'"
>
> —Eleanor Roosevelt

Financial Opportunity

This has to do with how *valued* you feel on the job. Employers depict your worth through the compensation they provide for it. How much you are paid for the work you do can greatly affect your wellness. It affects how you feel about yourself, your work, and your future, as well as how you live day-to-day. If you're being underpaid, it not only creates real-life problems, but it also erodes your self-esteem and creates resentment. Ways to protect and improve your financial wellness will be covered in Part IV.

Overall, it's important to remember that you can do what you love and still be tired or burned out. You can do what you love and still be excited about taking a break or working on your wellness. Focusing on improving how you spend one-third of your life is not a bad thing. Ultimately, this will allow you to be the best version of yourself at your job. Let's begin.

PART I

Boost Your Physical Wellness

Typically, your work environment, the physical demands required to do your job, or the aftereffects of both can detract from your overall physical well-being. If you're lucky, the physicality of your work and your work environment is basically neutral, though that is rarely the case in today's fast-paced, productivity-obsessed world.

This section will focus on your physical wellness at work by first identifying any problem areas, and then discussing ways you can feel healthy, safe, and stimulated while on the job. We'll begin by looking at potential negative impacts of your work environment; then explore ways you can keep your body alert and mind sharp while working; as well as things you can do at home to prepare yourself for functioning at peak capacity, while also fostering health at work.

"When you feel cast down, despondent, fearful, paralyzed, go outdoors and breathe."

—Elizabeth Towne, *Practical Methods for Self-Development*

IDENTIFY NEGATIVE IMPACTS ON YOUR PHYSICAL WELL-BEING

Let's begin by identifying the negative impacts the current physical aspects of your work are having on your physical well-being. Review the following list of questions and think about how they reflect on your workplace. Use the space on the next two pages to jot down any concerns or thoughts that these questions bring up.

Highlight everything on this page that applies, then turn the page.

Do you have a long commute? How much does this add to your stress? Are there alternatives, such as staggering your hours, working remotely a few days a week, or using public transit or carpooling?

Is your workplace safe? List any safety concerns.

Is the air quality good, or polluted?

Does the temperature at your workplace seem too hot? Too cold?

Is your work environment quiet, or too loud?

Is the lighting adequate? Is your workspace or desk well lit? Do you get natural light there?

Is your work environment visually stimulating?

Does your work environment need cleaning or painting?

Are there aspects of your job that cause physical discomfort or pain?

Do you have adequate space to do your job?

Do you have all the tools you need to do your job?

Is your workstation supportive of posture? Does it minimize hunched shoulders, back strain, excessive lifting, carrying, standing, sitting, or computer strain?

Is your workload too demanding or exhausting?

Do you have sufficient break time?

Is downtime encouraged? Do you have adequate vacation or sick days?

Is there a place to sit quietly, walk, or rest your eyes?

Is there a kitchen available, or a refrigerator so you can bring healthy meals or snacks?

Are healthy snacks or drinks available?

What else causes physical distress in your workplace?

Using the items from the previous page, create a list of what either harms or doesn't contribute to your physical wellness.

_____

_____

_____

_____

_____

_____

_____

_____

_____

_____

_____

_____

_____

_____

_____

_____

_____

_____

_____

_____

_____

_____

Narrow down your list from the previous pages to your most essential requests. Pick out things that affect your physical wellness that can only be fixed or provided by your employer, manager, or supervisor, such as:

- Environmental improvements: ventilation, sound, sight, smell.
- Air purifiers or live plants to clean the air.
- Whatever equipment, space, or ergonomic desk/chairs you need.
- An adjustable desk for sitting/standing.
- Flexible work hours, additional downtime for breaks and vacations.
- A lighter workload, or additional help.
- Healthy choices in vending machines or the cafeteria.

What's on your list? Specify what you want, why it's essential, and how its implementation would benefit not only you but the company. Use the space here to brainstorm, then find a diplomatic way to ask for what you need and want. After all, if you don't ask, you never know what you might receive. Preface your requests with positive statements about your work environment, then ask if you may offer ideas on how it could be even better. Manage your expectations and anticipate a little red tape for any changes that cost the company money or alter the way things have "always been done." While your manager might not be able to accommodate every request, they might surprise you by offering a compromise.

_____

_____

_____

_____

_____

_____

_____

_____

_____

_____

_____

_____

_____

_____

_____

_____

_____

_____

_____

_____

While many aspects of a workplace's physical environment are the responsibility of your employer (heat, adequate light, timed breaks), you also share the responsibility of making your work environment more beneficial than detrimental to your health. On the following pages are some ways *you* can improve your well-being at work.

MAKE SURE YOUR WORKSPACE FOSTERS HEALTH

Once you've addressed the physical concerns with your employer—and whether they've agreed to make changes or not—it's time for *you* to act. Though every workplace is different, here's a list of possible solutions you can adopt to improve the physical aspects of doing your job:

- Pause every sixty to ninety minutes to stretch or move; this increases the blood flow in your body and brain (see Chapter 1 for some ideas).
- Arrive rested, focused, and ready to work (see Chapter 2).
- Add artwork to your workspace for visual stimulation.
- Add plants to help clean the air.
- Use good posture to protect your back and shoulders.
- Keep your computer at a safe distance to protect your eyes.
- If you need glasses, especially for work, keep your prescription updated.
- Look away from your computer every twenty minutes, preferably into the distance—and if possible, outside, where a glimpse of nature might also refresh your brain.
- Pause often to take slow, deep breaths to keep your brain alert.
- Play soft music or wear noise-reducing headphones or ear buds.

Which of the previous suggestions do you need or want to put into action? Create a to-do list and decide based on priority what needs to be done first, second, and so on.

CHAPTER 1

Move as Much as Possible

Occupations that require prolonged sitting or standing, coupled with repetitive movements and/or awkward postures, can cause far more than soreness and fatigue. Depending on your posture, work duration, and exertion level, your back, shoulders, neck, legs, and wrists can experience long-term stiffness and discomfort. Over time, these physical restrictions and demands can seriously impact your physical health. Prolonged sitting increases the risk of heart disease, diabetes, obesity, and even cancer. Prolonged standing may elevate the likelihood of developing work-related musculoskeletal disorders (WMSDs).

Whether you have a job that requires standing for long hours, sitting all day, repetitive movement, or physical endurance—or not—we all know that the more you move and stimulate muscles that aren't being used, the healthier you will be.

Look for ways to incorporate movement at work, such as:

- Once an hour, push your shoulders back and gently roll your neck in circles.
- Occasionally raise your ankles off the floor, flex your legs, and point your toes—at least five times.
- Stand up whenever it's feasible (while reviewing documents, chatting with a coworker, talking on the phone). Simply standing will improve circulation—and, as a bonus, burn more calories.
- If possible, take a break outside and enjoy the sights, sounds, and the opportunity to move.
- Do desk exercises, which we'll cover in the rest of this chapter.

Which of the previous suggestions can you immediately put into practice?

_____

_____

_____

_____

_____

_____

_____

_____

_____

_____

_____

What else could you do?

_____

_____

_____

_____

_____

_____

_____

_____

_____

_____

WALK WHENEVER POSSIBLE

There's a new mantra, "sitting is the new smoking," which is a good reminder to all of us about how constant sitting can be dangerous to our health. In fact, according to the Mayo Clinic, prolonged periods of sitting seem to increase the risk of death from cardiovascular diseases and cancer, as well as increasing the likelihood of developing obesity and diabetes. Thankfully, sixty to seventy-five minutes of moderately intense physical activity a day alleviated many of the negative effects; the researchers recommend taking a break from sitting (or not moving) every thirty minutes.

Alternating not moving with standing, walking, or any other movement as much as possible is a straightforward way to reverse the negative effects of sitting through most of your workday. Here are a few ideas for incorporating walking into your day that are possible in a variety of work settings. Highlight any of the ideas you can immediately commit to doing.

- Wear a fitness tracker that measures your steps (and keep ramping up its count).
- Keep a pair of sneakers or comfortable walking shoes with you.
- Park far away from your building.
- Take the stairs.
- Ask coworkers to join you for walks on breaks (accountability is a big motivator!).
- Fit in a walk after eating lunch, which has been shown to boost metabolism.
- Transfer phone calls to a headset or any Bluetooth hearing device and pace while chatting.
- Turn a meeting into a walking meeting (and head outside if possible).
- Instead of sending an email or picking up the phone, walk to the other person's office and have a face-to-face chat.
- Instead of checking your phone when you have some downtime, go for a stroll, even if it's just to use a water fountain or bathroom in another part of your building.

What else could you do to move more often throughout your workday?

_____

_____

_____

_____

_____

_____

_____

_____

_____

_____

_____

_____

_____

_____

_____

_____

_____

_____

Try a Balancing Act

Because stability balls don't have back support, when you sit on them for any length of time, your muscles have to activate to keep you stable. Sitting even briefly on a stability ball while working can improve your posture, stability, and core strength.

EXERCISE AT YOUR DESK

Even if you sit most of the day, you can sneak in a few minutes here and there to move your body. Here are a few simple exercises that can get your blood flowing and boost your energy:

Seated crunch: Sit on the edge of your chair, place your hands behind your head, balance your toes lightly on the ground. Keeping your spine straight, breathe in, tighten your abs, then slowly lean your torso toward the chair back, hold briefly, then crunch back up, release your abs, and breathe.

Leg lifts: While sitting, lift and straighten your right leg, point your toe while flexing your leg muscles, hold for five seconds, then lower. Repeat it five times. Do the same with your left leg.

Calf raises: Stand up, put your arms down by your side, lift up onto the balls of your feet, hold briefly, then down again. Repeat five to ten times. If you need to do so, hold onto the back of your chair for stability.

Chair squats: Using a stable chair (no wheels, preferably hard back), sit down fully on the seat (not the edge), then simply stand up, tighten your buttocks, hold for two seconds, then sit down again. If needed, use your hands to push against the chair to help stand but work toward doing the movement without using your hands. Repeat five times.

High knees: While sitting, lift your knees up and down as high and fast as you can, as if you're running in place. Doing this for a few minutes can give a boost of energy.

To work arms and shoulders: Keep small weights and resistance bands handy to use during breaks. Simple arm extensions—or raising your hands while holding a weight or using a resistance band—will loosen up shoulder, arm, and hand muscles.

Two-Minute Refresher

Take a brief walking break every hour. Set an alarm on your watch or phone, then get up, stretch, walk around, and drink water. Even if you can squeeze in only two minutes, a short walk will get blood and oxygen flowing to your brain and warm up your muscles.

Which of the previous desk exercises can you put into practice?

_____

_____

_____

_____

_____

_____

_____

_____

_____

_____

What other exercises could you do at work?

_____

_____

_____

_____

_____

_____

_____

_____

_____

_____

_____

Incorporate Desk Yoga

Doing yoga doesn't always need leotards, a mat, bolsters, or a huge space. Simple yet very beneficial poses and movements can be done while sitting in your desk's chair, at or near your desk, or in tiny spaces. Whenever attempting a modified yoga pose, make sure your chair is sturdy (no wheels!) and that your feet won't slide. For most poses, you'll move to the center of the chair, keeping your feet flat on the floor and a comfortable distance apart (so you feel supported).

To Relieve Stress, Gently Stretch Your Back

If you sit for long hours, this pose will help with neck and lower back pain. Stand up, place your feet hip-width apart, then soften your knees and bend over, allowing your upper body to drop, as if you are a rag doll. Fold your arms and use each hand to hold onto the opposite elbow or let both arms extend toward the floor. Now, just hang there, allowing gravity to gently stretch your neck and back muscles, as well as your hamstrings. Hold this pose for two to three minutes. If you're comfortable doing so, you can try a similar stretch by holding on to the back of your chair and bending forward at the waist until you feel the stretch between your shoulder blades and hamstrings.

Do a Seated Twist

To stretch your back and realign your spine, try a seated twist. Sit down, stretch out your right leg and bend your left knee at about forty-five degrees to the floor, keeping your left foot flat on the floor. Inhale and slowly twist your body (from the hips) toward your left leg. Bring your right hand over and press against your left knee and gently pull to enhance the stretch. Hold the pose for ten seconds. See if you can slowly turn your neck and head to the right to gaze in the opposite direction of the stretch. Hold the pose for sixty seconds, then return to the original position; pause briefly, then repeat on the opposite side.

Center Yourself with a Tree Pose

Tree pose is a balancing pose that can be done anywhere you are standing, even while pouring your morning coffee or collecting papers from the printer. Straighten your spine and place all your weight on one foot. When you feel balanced, raise your other foot up the side of the standing leg, until it rests at about your knee. Push down toward the floor, and, if you can, bring both palms together in front of your chest. It might help your balance to find a focal point fix your gaze on it. Breathe slowly in and out, holding the pose for a few minutes, then repeat with the other leg.

Relax Your Lower Back with an Open Chest Stretch

Chest openers are excellent for counteracting the effects of prolonged hours of sitting at a desk or working on a computer. It's basically a slow backbend, which can be done sitting down or standing up. Straighten your spine, then slowly arch your back backwards, from the waist. Place a hand on each hip, then look up toward the ceiling and push your shoulders back to slowly open your chest. Inhale and exhale, holding the posture for ten seconds. Repeat five times.

If you have a place to lie down, place a bolster under your entire spine, or a firm pillow under your upper chest, then lay back and open your arms out to the side, stretching your chest. This should feel gentle and restorative, providing a shoulder release, while also supporting your spine. If you tend to slump, it's a great pose to practice often.

Relieve Tight Shoulders with a Modified Cat/Cow Pose

To relieve the tension that builds up in your upper back, shoulder, and neck, try a modified cat/cow pose that will both flex and extend your spine. Place your feet hip-width apart, flat on the floor. As you inhale, straighten your spine, and roll your shoulders slightly back. Place both hands on your thighs, and then as you exhale, slide your hand slowly toward your knees while rounding your spine and shoulders. Hold the pose for ten seconds. Inhale as you slowly roll up and straighten your spine again. Repeat this pose three to five times.

For a Gentle Shoulder and Back Stretch, Do a Seated Eagle Pose
Sit erect with a straight spine. Cross your right leg over your left at the knees. For an extra stretch, if comfortable, wrap your right foot around your left calf. (You can also do this with your feet flat on the floor if that's most comfortable.) Start with a modified version: bring both arms out to the side, then wrap them around yourself, like you're giving yourself a big hug. Pause for a few seconds, then open your arms wide, then hug yourself again, switching which arm is on top. Pause, then open again. Now this time, bring your arms in, right over left, and instead of hugging, bend them at the elbow where they cross over, with your hands raised and fingers pointing up (your hands will be in front of your face). Bring your forearms together and twist them as far as you can to press your palms together (if you can't quite reach, do the best you can). Gently lift up, while pushing your shoulders back. Inhale and hold briefly, then exhale as you lower your arms and release your hands. Pause and repeat on the other side.

To Loosen Up Your Shoulders, Do an Arm-Across-Chest Stretch
The arm-across-chest stretch is a wonderful way to loosen up your shoulders. While performing the exercise be sure to lower your shoulders if you experience pain. While sitting or standing, straighten your spine, then extend your right arm across your chest; use your left hand to hold your right elbow and gently pull your right arm more tightly across your chest. Hold for fifteen to thirty seconds. Repeat with your other arm. Do three to five times for each shoulder.

To Relieve Neck Pain, Do Neck Stretches
Stand or sit with your feet hip-width apart. Look straight ahead, then slowly tilt your head to the right, as if trying to touch your ear to your shoulder (but keep your shoulder down). If it's comfortable, place your right hand on your head and just let the weight of it push your head downward, stopping if it hurts. Hold for ten seconds. Repeat on the other side. Do three or four on each side, until your neck feels better.

Get Coworkers Moving

Invite coworkers for a group fitness program as a fun way to improve your physical health, bond, and blow off steam after working hours. Try bowling or pickleball, for example, or anything that helps relieve stress, fosters bonding, and provides movement.

CHAPTER 2
Come to Work Prepared

It might seem counterintuitive, but wellness at work begins with wellness at home. It's your responsibility to show up for work refreshed and prepared. This means practicing healthy habits, such as maintaining a balanced and nutritious diet, limiting or avoiding alcohol consumption (and drugs), and making sure you get adequate restorative sleep.

GET SUFFICIENT REM SLEEP

Adults need at least seven hours of sleep every night, but it's really the quality of sleep that affects how rested you feel in the morning. While you sleep, your body and brain progress through four stages of sleep. The first two are light stages that help your body and brain ease into a deeper sleep. Stage three is deep sleep, when your brain waves slow down, making it harder for you to wake up. During this stage, your body repairs itself, works on growth and development, boosts your immune system, and builds up energy for the next day.

The fourth stage is the essential rapid eye movement (REM) sleep. It usually begins about ninety minutes after you fall asleep. During REM sleep, your brain activity increases, your eyes dart around quickly, and your pulse, blood pressure, and breathing speed up. This is also when you do most of your dreaming. REM sleep is important for learning and memory. It's when your brain processes all the information you've absorbed during the day and either discards it or stores it in your long-term memory.

You go through these stages multiple times throughout the night, but are you getting enough cycles?

Common signs you need more sleep

Feeling drowsy or falling asleep during the day

Falling asleep within five minutes of lying down

Needing short periods of sleep during waking hours

Needing an alarm clock to wake up on time every day

Feeling groggy throughout the day

Difficulty getting out of bed every day

Mood changes and forgetfulness

Trouble focusing on a task

Sleeping more on days you don't have to get up

Lack of sufficient sleep may cause

Memory problems

Feelings of depression

Lack of motivation

Irritability

Slower reaction times

A weakened immune system

Stronger feelings of pain

High blood pressure, diabetes, heart attack, and/or obesity

Trouble solving problems and making decisions

How many hours a night do you sleep? Do you wake up feeling rested? Do you feel awake and alert throughout your day? If not, write about what's causing disruption to your sleep schedule.

_____

_____

_____

_____

_____

_____

Have your sleep habits changed recently? If so, how and why?

_____

_____

_____

_____

_____

_____

> ## "Having peace, happiness, and healthiness is my definition of beauty. And you can't have any of that without sleep."
>
> —Beyoncé, musician and entrepreneur

> "The reasons we can't sleep at night are usually the same reasons we don't truly live during the day."

—Michael Xavier, author

What contributes to you not getting sufficient sleep?

_____

_____

_____

_____

_____

_____

_____

_____

_____

_____

_____

_____

_____

_____

_____

_____

Tips for Improving Sleep Habits

If you're having trouble falling asleep or sleeping seven to nine hours a night, here are some practices that might help:

- Make sure you allot sufficient time to sleep. (If you know you have to get up at six in the morning, don't stay up to binge an entire series.)
- Go to bed and get up at the same time every day, even on weekends.
- Keep your bedroom dark, quiet, and at a comfortable temperature. Use it only for sleep, sex, and quiet activities like reading.
- Don't watch TV in your bedroom.
- Stop using tablets or cell phones at least one hour before bed.
- Spend a quiet hour before bedtime—put aside all electronics, dim the lights, and listen to an audiobook or soft music, if it helps calm you.
- Employ soothing and calming scents like a lavender eye mask or room spray.
- Stop eating at least three hours before bed.
- Avoid caffeine and alcohol in the evening; opt for herbal tea instead.
- Don't do vigorous or strenuous exercise just before bed (three hours earlier is fine, or light exercise up to one hour before bed); take a hot bath or shower to induce sleep.
- If you're in bed but not falling asleep, get up and do something quiet, like reading, until you feel sleepy.
- Journal before bed, writing out anything that might be keeping your brain buzzing. Making a to-do list for the next day sometimes helps.
- If you nap during the day, make sure it's no more than thirty minutes at a time. A little while after lunch is the best time to nap, when energy levels tend to dip.

If you've tried all of the previous tips and are still having trouble sleeping, talk to your doctor to make sure a medical condition, or a medication you're taking, is not contributing to your sleep problems.

> # "It is a common experience that a problem difficult at night is resolved in the morning after the committee of sleep has worked on it."

—John Steinbeck, author

Reframe How You Think about Bedtime

Julie Morgenstern, author of *Time Management from the Inside Out: The Foolproof System for Taking Control of Your Schedule—and Your Life*, said that if we think of sleep as the last thing we do at night, we're more likely to push it off—staying up to scroll TikTok or finish our to-do list. Instead, she suggests thinking of bedtime as a head start on the upcoming day. "Reframing rest as a new beginning rather than the tail end of the day can inspire better sleep habits," she notes.

EAT A HEALTHY BREAKFAST

The best way to give your body the energy—*and your brain the focus*—it needs for the day is to eat a filling and nutritious meal first thing in the morning. A healthy breakfast that will fire up your brain and provide stamina throughout your day doesn't have to be complicated.

Avoiding sugary cereals, breads, or pastries and focusing on protein, whole grains, and healthy fats (nuts and avocado, for example) is a good start; it will help you stay fuller for longer and avoid sugar crashes. Great options include Greek yogurt with granola, fruit, and/or seeds; eggs with whole-grain toast or avocado; oatmeal or overnight oats with raisins and nuts; a protein smoothie with fruit; peanut butter on whole-grain bread.

Remember that what you use to fuel your body and brain can make an enormous difference in how well you work, how you interact with others, and how tired you feel at the end of the day.

List five healthy breakfasts you do eat or could eat each week:

1. _____
2. _____
3. _____
4. _____
5. _____

To avoid feeling rushed, what could you prepare, or at least prep, the night before?

1. _____
2. _____
3. _____

EAT WELL AT WORK

In addition to eating a healthy breakfast, if you want to perform at your peak capacity, it's important to eat well while at work. Even if you tend to go out for work lunches, there are plenty of ways to improve nutrition during the workday, such as:

- Instead of relying on restaurants, cafeterias, or takeout for lunch, prepare nutritious home-cooked meals in advance, and bring healthy snacks such as: oatmeal packets, yogurt, fruit, nuts, pre-cut veggies and dip, sliced apples and peanut butter, or hummus and whole-grain pita chips.

- Avoid sugary drinks and too much caffeine. Caffeine isn't necessarily bad for you, but too many cups of coffee a day can leave you feeling tired and frazzled. Aim for two cups maximum, or dose down the caffeine by adding decaf to your mix in the afternoon. Or drink herbal tea.

- Stay hydrated. Keep a water bottle with you or a small thermos at your workstation. Sometimes when you think you're hungry, you are actually just thirsty.

Which of the above can you implement immediately? How specifically will you do so?

Brainstorm other ideas, focusing on ones that you think you'd enjoy most.

_____

_____

_____

_____

_____

_____

_____

_____

_____

_____

Engage Your Coworkers

A wonderful way to motivate and keep yourself accountable is to engage your coworkers in a plan to eat healthier. Suggestions include:

- Encourage sharing recipes and healthy potlucks.
- Suggest a fruit and vegetable exchange.
- Support each other in to reach your individual nutritional goals.
- Offer to take (or host!) a healthy cooking class.

You could all band together to request healthy snacks or lunches (if your company provides them). Or go on a once-a-week lunch date together in which you discuss your healthier eating stressors, habits, and goals.

PART II

Improve Your Emotional Wellness

The atmosphere in the workplace greatly affects any sense of wellness. A toxic and stressful work environment can trigger a host of problems, including a slump in employee morale, communication breakdowns, and mental and emotional distress.

Learning how to set the parameters for what you need to feel safe and happy in your work environment—as well as learning how to better manage your own emotions and how to extend compassion and empathy to yourself (and your coworkers)—will help you cope with challenging emotions and situations.

"People with well-developed emotional skills are also more likely to be content and effective in their lives, mastering the habits of mind that foster their own productivity; people who cannot marshal some control over their emotional life fight inner battles that sabotage their ability for focused work and clear thought."

—Dr. Daniel Goleman, *Emotional Intelligence*

Workplace Stress Is Real

A Mental Health America survey on workplace health of more than five thousand employees across seventeen industries in the United States found:

- 86 percent of respondents felt emotionally drained from their work;
- 99 percent of those respondents agreed that their workplace stress affects their mental health (71 percent strongly agreed);
- nearly 1 in 4 employees experienced the more severe signs of burnout, including reduced professional efficacy and cynicism toward coworkers and their jobs; nearly 60 percent felt their supervisors did not provide emotional support to help manage their stress;
- nearly 60 percent did not know what company-managed resources were available to them for emotional support;
- and more than half (56 percent) of employees spent time looking for a new job.

HOW ARE YOU FEELING AT WORK?

The first step in improving your emotional wellness at work is to assess how you're feeling when you're there. Rate your current emotional state from 1 to 10, with ten being either your optimum state or the highest level of discomfort. Where are you on the scale of feeling:

Energized and focused?	1	2	3	4	5	6	7	8	9	10
Exhausted and overwhelmed?	1	2	3	4	5	6	7	8	9	10
Alert and eager?	1	2	3	4	5	6	7	8	9	10
Sluggish and irritated?	1	2	3	4	5	6	7	8	9	10
Creative and responsive?	1	2	3	4	5	6	7	8	9	10
Fully seen and appreciated?	1	2	3	4	5	6	7	8	9	10
Motivated and rewarded?	1	2	3	4	5	6	7	8	9	10
Distracted and unproductive?	1	2	3	4	5	6	7	8	9	10
Abused and neglected?	1	2	3	4	5	6	7	8	9	10
Valued and respected?	1	2	3	4	5	6	7	8	9	10

Take a few minutes and create a list of what you've primarily been feeling at work. Presumably, you've picked up this book because it's not been going well, so here's where you can spill out your frustrations. Identify what you've been feeling and why.

> **"Happiness is not dependent on circumstances being exactly as we want them to be, or on ourselves being exactly as we'd like to be. Rather, happiness stems from loving ourselves and our lives exactly as they are, knowing that joy and pain, strength and weakness, glory and failure are all essential to the full human experience."**
>
> —Dr. Kristin Neff, *Self-Compassion*

What Causes Burnout?

According to the World Health Organization, burnout is defined as a syndrome resulting from chronic workplace stress that has not been successfully managed, characterized by three dimensions:

- feelings of energy depletion or exhaustion;
- reduced professional efficacy;
- and increased mental distance from one's job, or feelings of negativism or cynicism related to one's job.

Common factors that contribute to burnout include:

- overwhelming workload;
- long working hours;
- chronic staff shortages;
- an aggressive administrative environment;
- and a lack of support from management.

CHAPTER 3

Is Your Workplace Toxic?

It's entirely possible that you take the stoic approach to work: you go in without emotional baggage, do your job to the best of your ability and with satisfaction, you get along well with your coworkers, and you go home without giving work a second thought. But since you're reading this book, it's more than likely that *something* is bugging you. On the previous pages, you wrote about how you're feeling at work, but let's try to determine exactly what is causing you to be unhappy or stressed. Often, it's a toxic environment that causes your distress, which can include:

- Ineffective management or micromanagement
- Lack of support
- Lack of transparency; secrecy
- Poor communication
- Resistance to change; intractable
- Lack of stimulation; underutilization
- Stagnation; no opportunities for advancement
- High employee turnover; understaffed
- Unrealistic expectations or deadlines
- Too much conflict, tension, or stress
- Bullying or harassment
- Blame culture; failure to take responsibility
- Lack of recognition; inadequate salary
- Unequal treatment; playing favorites
- Work/life imbalance

Highlight all the items above that apply to your current work environment.

What is missing from this list that you deal with on a regular basis?

_____

_____

_____

_____

_____

_____

_____

_____

_____

Which items, from the previous lists, can be improved?

_____

_____

_____

_____

_____

_____

_____

_____

_____

_____

_____

Which ones must be improved for you to stay?

_____

_____

_____

_____

_____

_____

Which ones will you commit to addressing, and how will you address them?

_____

_____

_____

_____

_____

Why You Need Support

According to a Mental Health America survey, when a supportive manager values their identity, 84 percent of employees feel mentally and emotionally safe in that workplace. Because they feel supported and safe, 85 percent report being comfortable asking for promotions or providing feedback to their managers. In an almost total flip, among those who have managers who are _not_ supportive, 83 percent don't feel safe in their environment and 82 percent would not recommend it as a place to work.

PINPOINT CONTRIBUTORS AND DETRACTORS

It's important to examine aspects of your work that benefit or detract from your well-being. You can't launch an emotional wellness plan until you know what needs your attention the most. These contributors and detractors could be something you do, or don't do, as well as something your employer or coworkers do, or don't do. Consider the following categories so you can begin to pinpoint what needs to be reinforced or addressed for improving your workplace wellness:

- **Catalysts**: Policies, or actions taken by you or others, that directly support your work.
- **Nourishers**: People, events, or policies that show respect, or offer words of encouragement, that bolster your ability to work.
- **Inhibitors**: Policies, or actions taken by you or others, that actively hinder your ability to work.
- **Toxins**: *Persistent* aspects (people, situations, policies, or events) that discourage, sabotage, or undermine your ability to work.

List five catalysts present in your workplace that directly support your work.

1.

2.

3

4.

5.

What can you do to maintain or boost the catalysts?

_____

_____

_____

_____

_____

_____

_____

_____

_____

_____

What other catalysts would make you feel healthier and happier at work?

_____

_____

_____

_____

_____

_____

_____

_____

_____

_____

List five events, people, policies, or situations that nourish you at work.

1. _____

2. _____

3. _____

4. _____

5. _____

How do these specific events, people, policies, or situations nourish you at work?

_____

_____

_____

_____

_____

_____

What other types of events, people, policies, or situations would feel nourishing?

_____

_____

_____

_____

_____

List five actions that regularly hinder or inhibit your ability to feel safe, healthy, and happy at work.

1. _____

2. _____

3. _____

4. _____

5. _____

Who or what regularly causes these inhibiting situations or actions to occur?

_____

_____

_____

_____

_____

_____

_____

_____

_____

_____

_____

_____

_____

What could *you* do to improve each situation?

_____

_____

_____

_____

_____

_____

_____

_____

_____

What *specifically* would you need improved?

_____

_____

_____

_____

_____

_____

_____

_____

_____

List five toxins at work that leave you feeling demoralized.

1. _____

2. _____

3. _____

4. _____

5. _____

Who or what brings about these toxins?

_____

_____

_____

_____

_____

_____

_____

_____

_____

_____

_____

_____

_____

_____

_____

What can you do to make sure they stop?

_____

_____

_____

_____

_____

_____

_____

_____

_____

_____

_____

Now, list _specific actions_ **you can take to combat inhibitors and toxins, while boosting catalysts and nourishers.**

1. _____

2. _____

3. _____

4. _____

5. _____

6. _____

7. _____

8. _____

Envision your ideal work situation and jot down any and all crucial elements.

_____

_____

_____

_____

_____

_____

_____

_____

_____

_____

If these don't yet exist, how can you put them in motion?

_____

_____

_____

_____

_____

_____

_____

_____

_____

_____

Don't Let Depression Go Unchecked

Research on mental health in the workplace, published in the *Journal of Occupational and Environmental Medicine*, revealed that nearly 86 percent of employees treated for depression report improved work performance; and in some studies, treatment of depression has been shown to reduce absenteeism and presenteeism (being present but not alert, focused, or productive) by 40 to 60 percent. If you're depressed, first attempt to change whatever is causing your depression, and if that doesn't work, talk to your doctor so you can work as a team to find solutions.

SET AND MAINTAIN FIRM BOUNDARIES

To avoid emotional burnout and protect your physical, mental, and emotional wellness, you need to establish and maintain firm boundaries at work, as well as between work and home. Setting boundaries requires:

- Complete awareness (rather than ignoring or denying problems in the workplace, recognizing and owning them);
- a willingness to be clear about expectations, those of yourself and from others;
- and what you are and aren't comfortable with in specific situations—and setting parameters around expectations.

When setting boundaries, it's important to be clear both on what you want and what you need; then use assertiveness and clarity when communicating the specific boundaries you require.
Basically, work boundaries are:

- A way to protect you preserve your physical, mental, and emotional energy.
- Guidelines to help you live according to your values and standards.
- A limit that defines how you relate to someone or something.
- Physical, mental, or emotional lines that cannot be crossed:
  - **Physical boundaries** are your workspace (your work area, your desk), the physical separation allocated between you and coworkers, or being asked to do things beyond your physical capacity, and so on.
  - **Mental boundaries** are related to high expectations, excessive workloads, unrealistic deadlines, too much pressure, long work hours, after-work emails that require responses, and so on.
  - **Emotional boundaries** are related to how you feel, whether your coworkers respect your feelings, and how something or someone's behavior affects you. Emotional boundaries would be weak or nonexistent if a supervisor speaks in a belittling manner, coworkers take advantage of your good nature, or the boss chastises you in front of coworkers, and so on.

"Let all your things have their places; let each part of your business have its time."

—Marie Kondo, *The Life-Changing Magic of Tidying Up*

In order to set boundaries, first consider the following questions:

YES NO SOMETIMES

☐ ☐ ☐ Are there parameters in your workplace that preserve and protect your physical health?

☐ ☐ ☐ Are there parameters that protect your energy and ability to fulfill job expectations?

☐ ☐ ☐ Are there parameters that protect your ability to focus?

☐ ☐ ☐ Are there parameters in place that protect your mental and emotional health?

☐ ☐ ☐ Are supervisors and coworkers respectful?

☐ ☐ ☐ Do you often feel misunderstood, chastised, or abused?

☐ ☐ ☐ Are there coworkers (or bosses) who consistently step over your boundaries?

☐ ☐ ☐ Are there knowable expectations?

☐ ☐ ☐ Are workload expectations reasonable and doable?

☐ ☐ ☐ Is your workload excessive and unrealistic?

☐ ☐ ☐ Are you given sufficient time and space to meet expectations?

☐ ☐ ☐ Are you often under unrealistic or even punitive deadlines?

☐ ☐ ☐ Is there a clear chain of command?

☐ ☐ ☐ Is there a resource manager for airing grievances?

☐ ☐ ☐ Is there a clear work/home separation?

☐ ☐ ☐ Do you have control of your workstation?

☐ ☐ ☐ Is your time respected, or are others always impinging on your ability to focus?

☐ ☐ ☐ Do you often feel drained while working or after work?

☐ ☐ ☐ Are you constantly under deadline pressure?

☐ ☐ ☐ Do your coworkers regularly distract you?

☐ ☐ ☐ Are there too many meetings?

☐ ☐ ☐ Is your phone constantly ringing, or your email constantly pinging?

☐ ☐ ☐ Are others constantly infringing on your time?

☐ ☐ ☐ Are you often working through your lunch hour or breaks?

Using the previous questions as reference, make a list of specific issues that affect your ability to do your job well or that deplete your energy, confidence, job satisfaction, or physical health.

_____

_____

_____

_____

_____

_____

_____

_____

_____

_____

_____

_____

_____

_____

_____

_____

_____

_____

_____

_____

_____

_____

_____

Whatever you've pinpointed as your primary drains are where you need to establish boundaries. Brainstorm ideas for boundaries you could create that would address the specific problems you've listed above. Identify what you need others (and yourself) to do in order to recognize, protect, and respect your physical, mental, and emotional health, your values, your priorities, and your aspirations.

Now, write down in clear, declarative sentences how you will tell your coworkers or boss about your desired boundary. For example: "Unless we are in an emergency situation, I will be shutting off my phone and email after hours so that I may spend time with my family before bedtime. I will address anything that comes in during that time first thing in the morning." Practicing will help you present your requests in a clear, respectful, and empowered way. Remember that you're asking them to accommodate your needs and wants, but also that you have every right to ask for boundaries.

Are Your Boundaries Showing Respect?

Boundaries are the primary way you respect yourself and your time, with the goal of facilitating a healthier and more productive environment for you. It's also important that your boundaries show respect for your coworkers. Here's a checklist to see how you're doing on both aspects:

Do You Respect Yourself?

I ask for what I need.

I address any ongoing problems.

I find allies and neutralize adversaries.

I speak up when boundaries are crossed.

I ask for and accept help.

I ask for fair compensation.

Do Your Respect Your Coworkers?

I am clear in my communications.

I respect their boundaries.

I am cooperative and courteous.

I reciprocate kindness.

I regularly express appreciation.

I make efforts to heal problematic relationships.

> **"Keep your phone at least ten feet from your workstation during the day, off your nightstand at night, and turn off alerts and push notifications all the time."**

> —Dr. Aditi Nerurkar, *The 5 Resets*

LIMIT PHONE USAGE

When at work, but more particularly when not at work, it's essential to set boundaries around your availability. Cell phones and texting have created opportunities for coworkers and supervisors to reach out at any time, but that constant availability crosses that important borderline of separation between work and home. According to Nedra Glover Tawwab, author of *Set Boundaries, Find Peace: A Guide to Reclaiming Yourself*, being always available by phone contributes to burnout. "You have the right to be unavailable," she writes. She suggests the following strategies to limit phone usage:

- When home, plug your phone in at a fixed location, such as on a table in the hallway or in the kitchen, and only go to it when someone calls.

- When engaging in long phone conversations or listening to podcasts or audiobooks, use wireless earphones to avoid always having the phone on your person. This limits how many times you reach for your phone to relieve momentary boredom.

- Turn off notifications when you need to concentrate or need time to decompress.

- Unless you really need to take the call or respond to a text, let it go to voicemail or respond to it later. Immediately jumping to answer every text or phone call contributes to burnout.

Highlight which of the above strategies you can immediately adopt.

Don't Reach for Your Cell Phone

Oliver Burkeman, author of *Four Thousand Weeks: Time Management for Mortals*, believes we look for distractions at work when whatever we're working on triggers an unpleasant emotion, such as boredom, fear of not being able to complete the task at hand, or concern about not having enough time. To escape those feelings, we take refuge in scrolling on our phones. To conquer the pull that social media companies definitely encourage, he says it's helpful to remember that "the idea of distraction starts inside us," which means *you're in charge*. When uncomfortable emotions arise, he recommends that you focus on recognizing whatever feelings have caused discomfort, which will quiet your desire for escape.

When are you most vulnerable to distraction and likely to pick up your phone? What triggers you to disconnect from what you're doing?

> **"Remind yourself that your real life is here in your physical surroundings and talking to people and doing things. Make social media somewhere you go instead of the place you live."**

—Oliver Burkeman, *Four Thousand Weeks*

Take Tech Breaks

It's hard to get anything done when your computer or phone is pinging with notifications, emails, or texts. When you need to focus, turn off notifications so you can keep your attention on the task at hand. If necessary, once an hour give yourself one to two minutes for checking your email and phone. You may find that longer and longer tech breaks help you get a lot more done and feel less pressured or overwhelmed. If at all possible, do not view or respond to emails or texts outside of work. Or, only check them once between dinner and bedtime and let any response that can wait, wait.

REPLACE SELF-CRITICISM
WITH SELF-COMPASSION

Self-criticism would be saying or thinking: "It's my fault" or "I'm incompetent" or "I'm always wrong." Self-compassion would be saying or thinking: "I fell short on this particular assignment, but I'm growing and learning every day." Self-criticism fosters negativity and a self-defeating attitude; self-compassion fosters *positivity* and *resilience* by focusing on how you can grow and do better in the future. Self-criticism becomes a soul-crushing habit; self-compassion opens you up to growth and learning.

Self-compassion requires greater awareness of your surroundings and how your body feels. The more self-knowledge you possess, the more you'll be able to objectively view what's truly happening, your thoughts about it, and how to respond. It's basically offering yourself the same level of kindness and respect you would to someone you admire. (By the way, this is true outside of work, as well.) Here's how to develop self-compassion:

1. Treat yourself with kindness and respect.
2. See mistakes as opportunities to grow.
3. Replace self-criticism with positive self-talk.
4. Recognize and express gratitude for everything that goes well.
5. Offer yourself appreciation for trying your best.
6. Reward yourself for your progress.

What is a mistake from your past you're still thinking about? What actionable steps can you take to forgive yourself for it and grow from the experience?

_____

_____

_____

_____

_____

_____

_____

_____

What consistently makes you feel incompetent at work? How can you see this in a positive light and use the knowledge to grow?

_____

_____

_____

_____

_____

_____

_____

_____

_____

_____

Where do you most often feel challenged at work? What can you learn from this knowledge?

_____

_____

_____

_____

_____

_____

_____

_____

_____

_____

What positive things do your coworkers or supervisors say about you?

_____

_____

_____

_____

_____

_____

_____

_____

_____

What are you confident you do well? Be specific in giving yourself recognition.

List all the positive qualities that you bring to the workplace. Be specific and generous in your assessment.

CHAPTER 4
Regulate Your Emotions

Regulating your emotions in the workplace helps you be more resilient to change and adapt quickly to things that might throw you off your game. Emotional regulation skills help you recognize triggers, and thereby successfully navigate future uncertainty and change.

The ability to regulate your emotions doesn't mean that you don't feel them; it simply means that you regulate the intensity of an emotional experience and how you react to it. It doesn't mean suppressing or avoiding emotions, but using your awareness of them to recognize, respect, and then mindfully address what triggered them. With emotional regulation skills, you can influence which emotions you are willing to fully experience, how deeply you're willing to feel them, and *how* you express them.

> **"Understanding emotions is a journey. Possibly an adventure. When it's finished, we may find ourselves someplace new, someplace unexpected, somewhere, perhaps, we had no intention of going. And yet there we are, wiser than before—maybe wiser than we wished to be. But there's no other way forward."**
>
> —Dr. Marc Brackett, *Permission to Feel*

Signs that You're Regulating Your Emotions

You tamp down negative self-talk and ignore distracting thoughts.

You set aside unpleasant thoughts or emotions until you can be more objective.

You approach situations from multiple angles or viewpoints before reacting.

You manage your thoughts or feelings by objectively viewing and reframing the situation.

You put situations into context before reacting.

You consider multiple coping options before deciding how to respond.

Signs that You Need Emotional Regulation

You get easily distracted by, and obsessed with, upsetting thoughts or feelings.

Your thoughts and emotions interfere with your ability to focus.

You're highly sensitive and either lash out or withdraw when hurt.

When triggered, you have difficulty managing your emotions.

You feel like you easily lose control over your thoughts and emotions.

You find it hard to let go of intrusive thoughts or emotions.

How are you doing when it comes to emotional regulation? What are you doing to support your emotional health at work?

_____

_____

_____

_____

_____

_____

_____

_____

_____

_____

What consistently causes you the most problems?

_____

_____

_____

_____

_____

_____

_____

_____

_____

_____

What often triggers an unwelcome emotional response in you at your workplace?

_____

_____

_____

_____

_____

_____

_____

_____

_____

Did something happen recently that made you feel small, undervalued, or dismissed? What happened? How did you respond?

_____

_____

_____

_____

_____

_____

_____

_____

_____

Current emotional responses are often triggered by past experiences or emotional traumas. What past experiences or emotional earthquakes from your past get triggered at work?

_____

_____

_____

_____

_____

_____

_____

_____

_____

If you're easily distracted by unhelpful thoughts at work, what do they center on?

_____

_____

_____

_____

_____

_____

_____

_____

_____

When You Need Outside Help

Emotional regulation disorder occurs when someone consistently or chronically has difficulty adequately managing their emotions or keeping their reactions within an acceptable range. Also known as dysregulation, those who suffer from it, likely experience:

- Dramatic mood swings;
- Difficulty building and maintaining healthy relationships;
- Self-destructive behavior;
- Hypersensitivity;
- Frequent meltdowns or temper tantrums;
- Outbursts of emotions displaced onto someone who didn't cause the harm.

Emotional regulation disorder can also accompany other mental health issues. Disorders such as depression, stress, or borderline personality disorder often complicate emotional regulation. If your emotional distress is, or becomes, excessive, please seek outside help.

"Strength is about how you show up. It requires you to choose what energy and action you want to bring to a given situation. At its heart, strength is about self-management. It's not about controlling your emotions—it's about honoring them and choosing what you do next. It's hard to stay in control and get yourself off autopilot. It takes a lot of strength to move through the world with more thoughtfulness and intention. And sometimes it requires a heavy lift!"

—Darcy Luoma, *Thoughtfully Fit*

TECHNIQUES FOR REGULATING EMOTIONS

When you're caught in the maelstrom of emotion, it might seem impossible to have anything *but* those emotions. You might also feel resigned to experiencing these emotions anytime something doesn't go as planned or you're triggered. The good news is that anyone can learn techniques to better regulate their emotions. This book touches on many of those listed on the next two pages, as well as other specific techniques to easily protect your emotional health at work (see Chapter 5).

Identify and Reduce Triggers

When you experience something that reminds you of something painful that happened in the past, it can trigger strong emotions, out of proportion to what's currently happening. When you feel strong emotions at work, look for patterns or factors that are often present. Many of these arise from past injustices or deep-seated insecurities. When you know what they are, you can separate the present from the past and avoid overreaction.

Tune in to Your Body

Pay attention to how you are feeling, including whether you are feeling hungry or tired, which can exacerbate your emotions and cause you to interpret them more strongly. Once you address the underlying issue (e.g., hunger, exhaustion), it often calms you enough to avoid overreaction and *choose* a less-emotional response.

Verify the Facts

Before you jump to conclusions and express volatile emotions, gather the facts of each situation. Pause, step back, and consider whether you truly know what's going on and can objectively address it, or if you might be jumping to the wrong conclusion.

Flip Negative Thoughts to Positive Thoughts

Rather than berate yourself when you feel out of control, stop and immediately state something that counteracts your first, negative assumption, such as, "I am doing the best I can under these circumstances." Or, "They need more information before they make a judgment." Making a positive statement often deflects strong emotions, allowing you to better control how you respond.

Choose How to Respond

When a strong emotion arises, stop, breathe, and do a quick body scan to assess what you're really feeling. Before you speak, identify the true cause, why those particular strong feelings arose. Are they relevant to what just occurred, or are they triggered by your past? Often, if you stay in the present and quickly reassess, it'll defuse your feelings and you can choose a less confrontative response.

Focus on Positive Emotions

Most humans are primed to give negative emotions more credence than positive ones. Negative emotions like disgust, anger, and sadness tend to carry a lot of weight, while positive feelings like contentment, interest, and gratitude are quieter. Make a habit of questioning and defusing negative experiences and emotions, while noticing and savoring positive experiences and emotions. This will boost resilience and well-being, while assuming the worst less likely when something triggers a distressing emotion.

Seek help

If your distress goes on for a protracted time, emotional self-regulation becomes more challenging. There's no shame in needing extra support. It's fine to approach your Human Resources department to seek solutions. If that isn't an option or doesn't help, working with an objective therapist can help you gain the perspective you need and learn techniques to better regulate your emotions.

Avoid Coworker Venting

Even if you have a legitimate reason for feeling hyperemotional, it's not a good idea to vent frustrations with coworkers. While it may feel like "trauma bonding" and they may well be sympathetic, or even helpful, you never know if someone will overhear or later tell a supervisor what you said—in the heat of a moment. Instead of venting, use emotional regulation techniques to quiet your feelings. When your emotions have subsided, you can address whatever issue needs to be addressed, with whom it needs to be addressed, in a focused, calm, and respectful manner. Also, rather than allowing frustration to build, use this book to identify and address whatever is causing your ongoing distress.

TAKE OASIS MOMENTS

Practical Optimism: The Art, Science, and Practice of Exceptional Well-Being author Dr. Sue Varma reported that prioritizing short, revitalizing "oasis moments" during your workday—to do something you *choose* to do for enjoyment—provides a form of preventive care that can help fortify you throughout the day. These short breaks can be as simple as taking five minutes once or twice a day to stop working and focus solely on some form of relaxation or something that causes enjoyment.

It could be listening to your favorite song, reading a poem, looking out the window at nature, taking a short walk outside or around the office, or even making a quick coffee run. The point is to stop focusing on work and focus on something that brings you *pleasure* and provides five minutes of *relaxation*. Doing so has been shown to restore attention, reduce fatigue, increase vitality, and improve well-being and mood. Dr. Varma recommends taking your oasis moment before you feel tired, when recouping your energy level is easier; however, these moments can be restful at any time.

Taking this break, Dr. Varma adds, might also provide a sense of mastery and control. "You've made space and time for something that's beneficial," she says. "And you feel like you've achieved something for the day, similar to making your bed."

> ## "Rest is a highly therapeutic, untapped resource, and the positive effects can build over time."
>
> —Dr. Sue Varma, *Practical Optimism*

List five things you could do while taking a brief oasis from work.

1. _____

2. _____

3. _____

4. _____

5. _____

Be sure to notice how you feel when you take your breaks: Are you a little more refreshed? If not, try another activity.

Hold Off on Expressing Anger

In the heat of the moment, particularly at work, it's imperative that you hesitate before expressing anger. Firing off an angry DM, text, or email outlining your reasons for being angry may help you settle down, but *don't send them*! Wait until you've had time to get clarification on what happened and determine if your response will improve or further inflame the situation. It's best to sleep on it, then reread your diatribe the next day, when anger isn't clouding your judgment. If what you wrote the day before still feels accurate and worth expressing, perhaps let someone you trust take a look at it to help you decide if it needs to be modified or discarded.

CHAPTER 5
Better Manage Your Anxiety

Work-induced anxiety can be triggered by many things, including being overworked, underpaid, feeling undervalued, or being subject to a toxic work culture. It's characterized by excessive and enduring worry and nervousness about your job that eventually affects productivity, performance, and physical, mental, and/or emotional well-being. Some of the signs that you may be suffering from work-induced anxiety include:

- Difficulty concentrating and completing tasks;
- Missing deadlines because you're taking on too much;
- Focusing on the negative aspects of your job;
- Thinking about quitting your job often;
- Physical symptoms like headaches, fatigue, brain fog, or frequent sickness;
- Feeling easily frustrated with coworkers;
- Drop in work performance or decrease in productivity;
- Feeling dread when you have to go to work.

Feeling anxious is often spurred by a particular challenge and is perfectly normal. We all worry about our ability to complete a particular task, and feeling anxious often helps us focus and do our best work. But when anxiety isn't triggered by a particular challenge, becomes more generalized, and begins to impede your ability to function at your job, it's a problem.

If anxiety is impeding your ability to work at peak capacity or feel confident and capable at work, it helps to identify the cause. On the following page is a list of possibilities to consider.

Highlight anything in the following list that may be contributing toward increasing your anxiety levels at work:

- Undefined responsibilities
- Lack of instruction
- Lack of support
- Uncooperative coworkers
- Heavy-handed supervision
- Insensitivity of boss
- Excessive workload
- No advancement opportunities

- Low pay
- No appreciation or recognition
- Lack of teamwork
- Constant interruption
- Inefficiency
- Insufficient staff members
- Excessive hours
- Tedium

What else is causing you excessive anxiety at work?

_____

_____

_____

_____

_____

_____

_____

_____

_____

_____

_____

In each case on the previous page, is your anxiety protective and motivational or problematic and crippling?

_____

_____

_____

_____

_____

_____

_____

_____

If it's protective, what is it trying to tell you? What needs to change?

_____

_____

_____

_____

_____

_____

_____

_____

_____

_____

_____

If it's problematic and crippling, how can you immediately address it?

_____

_____

_____

_____

_____

_____

_____

_____

_____

_____

When you worry, is what you're worrying about based on reality, or on excessively exaggerated or unrealistic scenarios? Why?

_____

_____

_____

_____

_____

_____

_____

_____

_____

_____

If your anxiety seems excessive, unrealistic, or like an impediment, how can you realign your *mis*perception with reality?

_____

_____

_____

_____

_____

_____

_____

_____

_____

_____

If the worry is legitimate, how can you address it?

_____

_____

_____

_____

_____

_____

_____

_____

_____

_____

Is Your Stress Level Manageable or Crippling?

If it's manageable:

If it's crippling:

Change what you can. ·······························➤ Make immediate changes.

Ask management to institute ·······➤ Take a wellness break.
changes.

Adopt stress-management ·······➤ Look for a new job.
techniques.

How Do You Know If Work Anxiety Is a Problem?

The president of the American Psychiatric Association, Dr. Petros Levounis, noted that the presence of *constant* worry and fear is a signal you need help. Other signs include restlessness, a sense of fear or doom, increased heart rate, sweating, trembling, and trouble concentrating. Your work anxiety may be getting serious if work-related problems are bleeding into your personal relationships or home life. Maybe you find it hard to enjoy the weekends or your stress levels are causing you to be short-tempered or punishing toward your partner and/or children. If your attempts to self-manage anxiety about work aren't effective, it's time to reach out to a mental health professional.

> **"Some days, doing the best we can may still fall short of what we would like to be able to do, but life isn't perfect—on any front—and doing what we can with what we have is the most we should expect of ourselves or anyone else."**
>
> —Fred Rogers, television host and author

ARE YOU IN RETREAT MODE?

Dr. Luana Marques, author of *Bold Move: A 3-Step Plan to Transform Anxiety into Power*, notes that stressed people often feel compelled to deny what's happening and use retreat from responsibilities as an *avoidance strategy*, to feel temporary relief from or to put off whatever is making them anxious. This is not a productive strategy as the problems will still exist and may even worsen when not immediately addressed. Ways people retreat include:

- Cutting short difficult conversations
- Changing the topic
- Letting emails pile up
- Putting off small tasks
- Rescheduling unwanted meetings
- Scrolling through social media

What happens at work that often causes you to feel so anxious you consistently resort to avoidance?

Is it a belief that you're not good enough? If so, when did this begin? Is it a carry-over from past experiences? Is it relevant to your current job responsibilities?

Are you worried about being judged incompetent? If so, why? What skills are you lacking, if any? What can you do to increase your confidence?

Are there specific criticisms that leave you feeling worthless?

If specific criticisms leave you feeling woefully inadequate, is there a legitimate reason for you to feel that way? Or might this sensitivity stem from childhood experiences?

_____

_____

_____

_____

_____

_____

_____

_____

_____

_____

_____

Often what's perceived as criticism is feedback that hasn't been presented well. What are five things you do at work that have been criticized? Could any of these have been meant as encouraging feedback?

1. _____

_____

2. _____

_____

3. _____

_____

4. _____

_____

5. _____

_____

Once you identify any underlying fears that cause you to feel anxious at work, write three negative beliefs that have developed as a result of them, which you've consciously or unconsciously accepted about yourself.

1. _____

_____

_____

2. _____

_____

_____

3. _____

_____

_____

Now write a positive statement for each statement on the previous page that refutes those outdated attitudes. Use these positive statements as a way to rethink your own assessments.

1. _____

_____

2. _____

_____

3. _____

_____

Write five statements that you know are true about how well you do your job.

1. _____

2. _____

3. _____

4. _____

5. _____

"Journal writing, when it becomes a ritual for transformation, is not only life-changing but life-expanding."

—Jennifer Williamson, author

WRITE IT OUT

Writing in a private journal about what's causing you anxiety at work gives you a place and time to vent, specify the culprits, defuse reactionary emotional responses, and identify ways to address what causes you regular distress. If self-reflection becomes part of your daily routine, you'll soon pinpoint recurring frustrations, problematic situations (or people), and how your responses, or lack of responses, may be sabotaging your best efforts to get along with others, do your best work, and experience increased health and fulfillment while on the job.

Journaling on a regular basis will also help you identify areas for growth, brainstorm solutions, and even recognize your strengths. Plus, studies show writing in a journal can help reduce the effects of stress, anxiety, and depression, while increasing resilience.

Even if you keep all your insights to yourself, writing them down on a regular basis can significantly enhance your self-awareness. Consider it your special space to process emotions, channel growth, bolster creativity, and, ultimately, develop a deeper relationship with yourself. It's ideal to have a special journal set aside for this purpose. You can find a wealth of options at bookstores or online. Pick one that sparks passion or creativity, and you'll be more likely to pick it up and write in it.

Start here by writing about your current work situation, focusing on what is going well and what needs a fresh perspective or a new strategy. Use writing as a way to expel any negative emotions and reinforce positive ones. If your entries are primarily negative, use journaling as a way to brainstorm solutions.

Journaling Apps

If you don't want a physical journal, there are, of course, a multitude of apps you can use. Here are a few to consider:

- 5 Minute Journal
- Penzu
- Grid Diary-Journal, Planner
- Day One Journal: Private Diary
- TheJournal
- Wellnest Journal

> **"There is no single more powerful—or more simple—daily practice to further your health and wellbeing than breathwork. "**
>
> —Dr. Andrew Weil, physician and author

CALM YOURSELF WITH BREATH WORK

We all breathe, but often we do so unconsciously and insufficiently. Breathing exercises can provide a myriad of health and wellness benefits for both the mind and body. Conscious, focused breathing discourages the kinds of natural, shallow breaths (known as chest breathing) or the rapid breathing that can often signal, but also increase, anxiety. When stressed, simply pausing to focus on your breath and purposefully slowing it down can immediately and effectively bolster a sense of calm. Benefits of conscious, focused, deep breathing also include:

- Stress relief
- Improved focus and concentration
- Enhanced lung capacity
- Reduced blood pressure
- Balanced emotional state
- Improved sleep
- Detoxification
- Strengthened respiratory muscles
- Enhanced digestion
- Elevated mood

If you incorporate regular breathing techniques into your daily routines, you'll soon experience these benefits and improve your overall quality of life. The following pages outline specific breathing techniques you can use to calm and refocus yourself at work—or anywhere.

"Breathing in, my in-breath has become deep.

Breathing out, my out-breath has become slow.

Breathing in, I feel calm.

Breathing out, I feel at ease.

Breathing in, I smile.

Breathing out, I release all my worries and anxieties.

Breathing in, I dwell deeply in the present moment.

Breathing out, I know this is a wonderful moment.

Smile... There are more than three hundred muscles in our face, and when we know how to breathe in and smile, these muscles can relax. This is 'mouth yoga.'"

—Thich Nhat Hanh, "The Noble Eightfold Path"

Box Breathing

Box breathing, also known as square breathing, is a simple yet effective technique to relieve stress and enhance focus. All that is required is taking in and exhaling slow, deep breaths in a regular rhythm, following a "square" pattern.

1. Inhale; breathe in slowly through your nose for a count of four.
2. Hold your breath for a count of four.
3. Slowly exhale through your mouth for a count of four.
4. Wait for another count of four before inhaling again.
5. Repeat this cycle for a few minutes, gradually increasing the interval from four to higher numbers as you become more comfortable.

How did you feel while box breathing? Did it help you relax?

_____

_____

_____

_____

_____

_____

_____

_____

_____

_____

_____

_____

_____

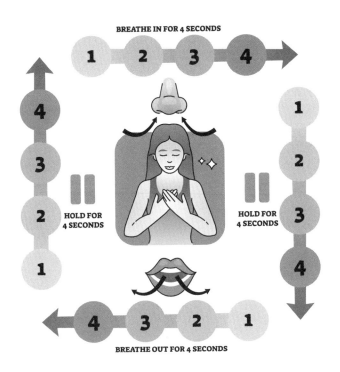

BREATHE IN FOR 4 SECONDS

1 2 3 4

4 3 2 1

HOLD FOR 4 SECONDS

1 2 3 4

HOLD FOR 4 SECONDS

4 3 2 1

BREATHE OUT FOR 4 SECONDS

"The practice is simply this: keep coming back to your breath during the day. Just take a moment. This will give your mind a steadiness and your breath a gracefulness... There's so much to let go of, isn't there? Your nostalgia and your regrets. Your fantasies and your fears. What you think you want instead of what is happening right now. Breathe."

—Rodney Yee, *Yoga: The Poetry of the Body*

Pursed Lip Breathing

Pursed lip breathing is an effortless way to improve ventilation, release trapped air from the lungs, and increase the amount of oxygen reaching them. It's particularly helpful if you suffer from respiratory conditions, but anyone can use it to promote deeper and more effective breathing. Regular practice of pursed lip breathing can help improve lung function, relieve shortness of breath, and encourage a calming effect on the mind and body.

1. Sit or stand up straight. Consciously relax your neck and shoulders. Do a shoulder or neck roll, if needed.
2. Take a deep breath in through your nose for a count of two.
3. Pucker or "purse" your lips, almost as if you are readying to blow out a candle, and then exhale slowly and steadily through your pursed lips for a count of four or more, doubling the time you took to inhale.
4. Continue this pattern for a few minutes, focusing on the sensation of the breath and ensuring the exhale is controlled and twice as long as the inhale.

How did pursed lip breathing feel? Is it something you can do at work?

_____

_____

_____

_____

_____

_____

_____

_____

_____

_____

_____

_____

_____

"Your confidence, your endurance, the vitality you require to live your life, the very essence of your life itself and your chi, or life energy, are stored in your breath."

—Catherine Carrigan, _The Little Book of Breathwork_

Breathe through Your Diaphragm

Diaphragmatic breathing—also known as deep breathing, abdominal breathing, or belly breathing—involves inhaling and exhaling from your diaphragm, the large muscle located just below your lungs. Doing so maximizes oxygen intake, promotes full oxygen exchange, and helps reduce stress and stabilize blood pressure. Regularly engaging in this deep breathing exercise can improve lung function, relax the body, and calm the mind, making it especially useful for those with anxiety. You may need to learn this at home, preferably while lying down. But once you've mastered the technique, you can modify it to a sitting posture at work; if it feels too awkward to do so, also refrain from putting your hands on your abdomen and chest.

1. Begin by lying (or sitting) in a comfortable position. Place one hand on your chest and the other on your abdomen.

2. Using your stomach muscles rather than your chest muscles, breathe in deeply through your nose. If you're doing it right, your abdomen rather than your chest will rise with the breath; the hand on your chest will remain as still as possible.

3. Purse your lips, use the hand on your expanded abdomen to press down as you slowly exhale. Again, the hand on your chest should remain mostly stationary.

4. Continue this pattern, taking your time with each breath and focusing on the rise and fall of your abdomen.

"If you want to conquer the anxiety of life, live in the moment, live in the breath."

—Amit Ray, author and yoga teacher

Did diaphragmatic breathing help calm any anxiety?

_____

_____

_____

_____

_____

_____

_____

_____

_____

_____

_____

_____

_____

_____

_____

_____

Alternate Nostril Breathing

Alternate nostril breathing is an ancient yogic breathing practice designed to balance the left and right hemispheres of your brain, clear energy channels, and promote a sense of calm and focus. Basically, it's using your right thumb or ring finger to hold one nostril closed while breathing in through the other, then releasing the closed side to slowly exhale out of it. With regular practice, you can extend the length of time you spend breathing this way. Doing so will enhance concentration, foster equilibrium, and rejuvenate your nervous system.

1. Sit upright in a comfortable position. As you do this technique, seek a slow, steady flow.

2. Rest your left hand on your leg (or desk) and clear your lungs by exhaling completely. Then use your right thumb to hold your right nostril closed.

3. Inhale slowly through your left nostril, then use your right hand's ring finger to hold your left nostril closed.

4. Release your right nostril and slowly exhale through this side.

5. Still holding your left nostril closed, slowly inhale through your right nostril.

6. Close your right nostril, release your left nostril, and slowly exhale through the left side. This completes one cycle. Continue this cycle for three to five minutes.

7. Finish with an exhale from the left nostril, then take a few moments to breathe normally, observing any changes in your state of mind or energy level.

How did alternate nostril breathing feel?

_____

_____

_____

_____

_____

_____

_____

_____

_____

_____

_____

_____

_____

_____

"Our breathing is designed to help us release any tensions that have become so much a part of us that we no longer sense their presence."

—Carla Melucci Ardito, somatic therapist, yoga teacher, and writer

4-7-8 Breaths

The 4-7-8 breathing technique is a simple practice that bolsters relaxation by reducing stress and anxiety, as well as promoting restorative sleep. Over time, the 4-7-8 breath will naturally tranquilize your nervous system.

1. Quietly breathe in through your nose for a count of four.
2. Hold your breath for a count of seven.
3. Slowly exhale with your mouth wide open for a count of eight, making a whooshing sound as you breathe out.
4. Repeat this cycle for four breaths initially, and with practice, extend it up to eight breaths at a time.

How did this form of breathwork feel? Do you feel calmer?

_____

_____

_____

_____

> **"When the breath is unsteady, all is unsteady; when the breath is still; all is still. Control the breath carefully. Inhalation gives strength and a controlled body; retention gives steadiness of mind and longevity; exhalation purifies body and spirit."**
>
> —*Gorakṣaśataka*

MEDITATE TO FOSTER INNER PEACE

We get so caught up in our own thoughts, worries, and external distractions, that finding moments of stillness and inner peace often seems impossible. Meditation is the practice of sitting quietly while allowing thoughts to come and go, simply recognizing and releasing them, without judgment. If you regularly meditate, you'll learn the very useful skill of quieting your thoughts and creating moments of peaceful restoration. Over time, meditating will help you keep your focus on what's happening in the present and better manage your emotions.

Benefits of a meditation practice extend far beyond the initial moments of tranquility:

- **Enhanced self-awareness.** Observing your mind without judgment provides valuable insights into your inner workings, while fostering self-acceptance and personal growth.
- **Reduced stress and anxiety**. The constant chatter of worries and anxieties are replaced by a sense of inner peace.
- **Increased sense of calm and tranquility.** If practiced regularly, meditation can help you find moments of stillness and serenity, even in the workplace.
- **Strengthened self-compassion.** As you become more aware of your thoughts and emotions, meditation often leads to more self-acceptance and compassion.
- **Improved focus and concentration.** It helps you enhance your ability to stay on task and avoid distractions.
- **Enhanced sleep quality.** The calming effects can aid in relaxing your mind and body, potentially making it easier to fall asleep—and stay asleep—throughout the night.
- **Deepened intuition and creativity.** As you quiet the mind and connect with your inner self, you might find ideas and insights flow more freely.

Which of the benefits on the previous page would immediately improve your workplace wellness? Briefly explain why you're having a problem with each one.

_____

_____

_____

_____

_____

_____

_____

_____

_____

_____

Brainstorm a strategy for improving them.

_____

_____

_____

_____

_____

_____

Research Bears It Out

Research comparing those who regularly meditate to those who don't found that people who establish a meditation practice report significantly higher levels of mindfulness, self-compassion, and overall sense of well-being, *plus* significantly lower levels of psychological symptoms, rumination, thought suppression, fear of emotions, and difficulties with regulating emotions. Regular meditation practice is also associated with enhanced cognitive flexibility and attentional functioning.

Create Space for Meditating

Meditation serves multiple purposes: it's a way to both clear and focus your mind before going to work; it's a way to relieve stress while at work; and it's a highly beneficial way to reduce stress as you transition from work to home, or from awake to asleep. Obviously, longer meditations are best done at home—unless your workplace provides a suitable space and a long enough break—but it's possible to meditate in as little as three minutes. Shorter ones are quite effective when you need a quick release or pick-me-up at work.

Having a special place at home for meditating is ideal, but anywhere you can be alone and not interrupted for 5 to 10 minutes will suffice. You can sit on the floor, or on a chair or couch, wherever you are comfortable. Some people like to use candles, crystals, or a sound device (singing bowls, chimes, a rattle) as part of their meditation ritual. Some people like to play soft music or nature sounds, and some like to access guided meditations online. Whatever helps you quiet your mind and transition from your busy life into meditation mode is fine.

Master Meditation Basics

The basics of meditation are simple:

- **You may want to set a timer for five to ten minutes** (keep the volume low so you don't startle yourself when it goes off). Choose a quiet place where you won't be disturbed. Sit comfortably, cross-legged on the floor, or on a chair or couch with your feet flat on the floor (to ground you), and your spine straight. You can also lie down if you prefer. If sitting, place your hands lightly on your thighs, palms up or down, or touch the tips of your thumbs with your index fingertips. Whatever feels most comfortable is fine.

- **Close your eyes and begin breathing slowly in and out**. As you do so, focus solely on the natural rhythm of your body as you inhale and exhale. Notice how your body feels as you draw the breath in, hold it, then slowly exhale. As you progress, draw in deeper breaths from your diaphragm, briefly hold them, and then slowly release them.

- **Every time your mind wanders** (which it will!), simply bring your focus back to your breath. You may have to do it frequently when starting out.

- **When your timer goes off, slowly open your eyes**. Take a few deep breaths and allow yourself to savor the stillness within you, then slowly stand and resume your day.

Once you've learned the basics of meditation, you might want to find guided meditations online or download apps, such as Calm or Elevate, to deepen your meditation.

> **"You say that you are too busy to meditate. Do you have time to breathe? Meditation is your breath."**
>
> —Ajahn Chah, Buddhist monk and author

How did meditating feel? What sensations did you feel?

_____

_____

_____

_____

_____

_____

_____

_____

What thoughts kept seeping in?

_____

_____

_____

_____

_____

_____

_____

_____

_____

_____

Were you able to release those thoughts and refocus on your breath?

_____

_____

_____

_____

_____

How can you incorporate meditation into your daily life?

_____

_____

_____

_____

_____

"The next time your phone rings, use it as a reminder to be mindful. Stay exactly where you are, and become aware of your breathing: Breathing in, 'I calm my body.' Breathing out, 'I smile.' When the phone rings the second time, breathe again . . . continue practicing breathing, and then pick up the phone."

—Thich Nhat Hanh, Buddhist monk, peace activist, and author

How Meditation Helps in the Workplace

Meditation can help you experience thoughts and emotions with greater balance and acceptance. It has also been shown to:

- Improve attention;
- Decrease job burnout;
- Improve sleep.

Ideally, your workplace would have a private, quiet space where you can take a break. If so, you can meditate for three to five minutes in relative isolation. In the event that a few coworkers want to join in, perhaps you can book a conference room when it's convenient for everyone. You can also do a quick meditation at your desk, even if it's simply focusing on your breath, as you breathe slowly in and out for two minutes.

On the following pages are some sample meditations you can do at your desk.

Try a Mindful Body-Scan Meditation

Another way to induce relaxation is to do a quick, mindful, body-scan meditation in which you pause to tune into your physical body. Doing so will help relieve any bodily tension, anchoring your mind in the here and now instead of letting it spiral into anxiety-inducing thoughts.

1. Begin by making yourself comfortable. Sit in a chair and allow your back to be straight, but not stiff, and keep your feet on the ground. Rest your hands gently in your lap or at your sides. Allow your eyes to close, or to remain open with a soft gaze.

2. Take several long, slow, deep breaths, in through your nose and out through your mouth. Feel your diaphragm expand as you inhale and relax as you exhale. Tune out any distractions and shift your attention to what's happening inside your body.

3. Now, as you inhale, bring your attention to your feet. Notice how they feel, perhaps wiggle your toes, and send your breath down to your toes, then back up again, releasing any tension as you do.

4. Proceed up your body, focusing on your legs, your abdomen, your chest, your shoulders, your arms and hands, and your head, setting free any tightness.

5. Do a few final, cleansing breaths, and then open your eyes.

Try a Mudra Meditation

A wonderful meditation for calming down and focusing that you can do at your workstation is a simple finger placement, or mudra, meditation that employs the specific sounds "Sa, Ta, Na, Ma," which represent the following:

- SA is birth, the beginning, infinity, the totality of everything that ever was, is, or will be.
- TA is life, existence, and creativity, which manifests from infinity.
- NA is death, change, and the transformation of consciousness.
- MA is rebirth, regeneration, and resurrection, which allows us to intentionally experience the joy of the infinite.

To use these sounds in meditation, you'll briefly press each of your four fingers to the thumb of the respective hand. With each finger, you will sing, whisper, or silently say "Sa," "Ta," "Na," and "Ma." The singing voice represents your voice of action, the whispered (or chanted) voice represents your inner mind, and silently "saying" the words to yourself represents your spiritual voice.

1. Take a few full, deep, cleansing breaths. Close your eyes and rest your hands gently in your lap, on your desk, or down your sides with palms facing up. Then, one at a time, touch each finger on both your hands to its respective thumb as follows:
2. Touch your index fingers to your thumbs, say "Sa," then release.
3. Touch your middle fingers to your thumbs, say "Ta," then release.
4. Touch your ring fingers to your thumbs, say "Na," then release.
5. Touch your pinkies to your thumbs, say "Ma," then release.
6. Repeat a few times, increasing in speed, until you feel both calm and focused.
7. Inhale deeply, wiggle your fingers, and shake your hands to release any pent-up energy.

"If you can't meditate in a boiler room, you can't meditate."

—Alan Watts, writer

BOOST AWARENESS THROUGH MINDFULNESS

Mindfulness began as a spiritual practice Buddhist priests adopted some 2,550 years ago. It's defined as simply paying attention in a particular way: on purpose, in the present moment, and nonjudgmentally.

Being mindful in the workplace means that you are simply paying attention to the situations happening in the present moment, in an open and accepting way. Because it encourages *introspective* awareness—with regard to your physical and psychological processes and experiences—it helps you pause before overreacting; it also helps you nonjudgmentally approach your work and your relationships with other colleagues and management.

With practice, you can develop an inward and outward awareness of what's going on with you, with others, and with your surroundings, in the present moment, sans judgment. It not only helps you see your thought process (so you can self-correct when necessary), but the nonjudgmental clarity it brings helps you make better decisions. Mindfulness in the workplace helps you keep an open mind and be more willing to listen and learn from others. It also fosters creativity by helping you be more receptive to thinking outside the box. Basically, you'll be a better version of you.

Because mindfulness practice trains your brain to focus solely on what you're doing in the present moment, it is the antithesis of multitasking. Studies have shown that people who try to multitask are less effective when they focus on two or more tasks, than they would be if they focused on one thing until it was done. Mindfulness helps train your brain to focus on one task at a time.

> **"Mindfulness is the ability to know what's happening in your head at any given moment without getting carried away by it."**
>
> —Dan Harris, *10% Happier*

The Many Benefits of Mindfulness

People who regularly practice mindfulness tend to:

- Live in the present moment.
- Have unusual awareness of the environment they are in and what is going on around them.
- Actively employ all their senses to observe people and their surroundings.
- Learn to focus on breath, which helps them feel grounded.
- Practice active listening.
- *Read* the room then use their observations to adjust their response.
- Practice meditation by simply finding time throughout the day to sit or lay down in a quiet space and focus on their breathing to reset their minds.
- Check in with themselves and pay attention to feelings when they occur, so they can identify and label them, and then decide how to respond.
- Show compassion for others and for themselves. They embrace how imperfect they are, which makes them more accepting of others.
- Remain curious, and tend to read, explore, debate, and listen more often.
- Avoid multitasking, with the awareness that they need to slow down in order to pay attention to more things.
- Align their thinking, their feeling, and their intuition, gifting them a sense of consistency and stability.
-

> "Mindfulness practice means that we commit fully in each moment to be present; inviting ourselves to interface with this moment in full awareness, with the intention to embody as best we can an orientation of calmness, mindfulness, and equanimity right here and right now."

—Jon Kabat-Zinn, PhD, originator of mindfulness-based stress reduction (MBSR) meditation

Mindfully Meditate

Mindfulness sounds complicated but it's very simple. It's even easier if you learn how to meditate first, and then use those skills to reach a meditative state. Once you're relaxed, mindfulness is achieved by quieting yourself and your brain, and then bringing all your focus to one thing. Some people identify a focal point, some stare at a candle, and some hold a sacred object, but whatever is handy and helps you focus will do. If your mind wanders (and it will!) simply release the thoughts (briefly envision them as butterflies or birds flying off into the stratosphere) and promptly bring your focus back to the object. Keep doing this until you can sustain your focus for at least five minutes.

Aim to practice mindfulness every day for about six months. Over time, you will likely find that it becomes so effortless, you slip into a mindful state without even realizing it. This will become an essential tool in your emotional and mental arsenal.

Practice Mindful Breathing

Mindful breathing simply means focusing on the sensations and rhythms of the process of breathing, making it something you can use at work when you're stressed or need to focus. It's accomplished by paying close attention to each inhalation and exhalation, to cultivate a deeper awareness of the present moment, and foster relaxation and clarity. Regular mindful breathing can help reduce stress, improve concentration, and foster a deeper connection with yourself.

1. Sit comfortably in a chair or on the floor and straighten your spine. You can also lie down, if preferred.

2. Close your eyes and focus solely on how breathing feels. Breathe slowly in and out, while noticing how breath feels when it enters your nostrils, fills your lungs, travels down to your diaphragm, and then slowly exits your body. Focus on the bodily sensations.

3. Also notice the rise and fall of your chest and abdomen with each breath. To enhance awareness, place your hands on either or both.

4. If your mind wanders, release the thoughts, and gently bring focus back to your breath.

5. Start with five minutes and, as you become more accustomed to the practice, gradually increase the duration.

This may seem simplistic at first, but practiced regularly, mindfulness meditation trains your brain to tamp down distractions and focus on what's happening in the now. One can practice mindfulness while doing simple tasks, like taking a bath, preparing a meal, planting flowers in the garden, or even taking a walk around the block. Simply keep your focus on your breath, how your body feels, what is happening in the present, and what you are observing and feeling related to whatever you are doing.

Start now, by trying a simple five-minute mindfulness meditation. As you become more comfortable, increase the amount of time you spend in mindfulness.

Were you able to feel more connected to the present moment? What thoughts arose? Were you able to restore focus on your breathing?

_____

_____

_____

_____

_____

_____

_____

_____

_____

_____

_____

_____

It Brings Emotional Mastery

Mindfulness encourages awareness and nonjudgmental acceptance of one's moment-to-moment experience, which becomes an effective antidote against psychological distress—rumination, anxiety, worry, fear, anger, and so on—many of which involve the maladaptive tendencies to avoid, suppress, or over-engage with one's distressing thoughts and emotions.

The Many Benefits of Mindfulness

In due course, a consistent practice of mindful meditation literally changes our brains, making them more flexible, focused, and more resilient to stress. Basically, mindfulness meditation:

- Quiets the amygdala and neurological connections to the medial prefrontal cortex, which are both responsible for fear, stress, and anxiety.
- Increases activity in brain regions associated with attention, awareness of how you feel, and sensory processing.
- Increases activation in processing of distracting events and emotions.
- Grows gray matter responsible for emotional regulation, planning, and problem solving.
- Increases cortical thickness, which improves learning and memory.
- Builds new pathways to the parts of the brain responsible for focus and decision making.

Meditation also stimulates your parasympathetic nervous system, which can abate indicators of stress in the body including lowered heart rate, reduced blood pressure, and fewer spikes in cortisol (the stress hormone).

Mindfulness has also been positively associated with psychological health, by increasing levels of positive affect, life satisfaction, vitality, and adaptive emotional regulation, and lowering levels of negative affect and psychopathological symptoms. In other words, it improves mental and emotional health, helping you feel happier and healthier overall.

Benefits of Mindfulness in the Workplace

Mindfulness has been shown to help people at work in the following ways:

You learn to pay attention. It teaches you to slow down and use all your senses—touch, sound, sight, smell, and taste—to process what's happening. This added focus helps you become more productive, creative, patient, and understanding.

You learn to live in the moment. Mindfulness enables you to be more aware of the importance of the present, as opposed to the past or the future, which reduces distractions and bolsters clarity.

You learn to stay fully conscious. Living in the moment pulls whatever activity you happen to be doing from the habitual part of your brain back to the conscious part of your brain, allowing you to *consciously choose* how you react and behave.

It bolsters acceptance. To be mindful means to accept this present moment just as it is, which helps you acknowledge the truth of how things are now before deciding what to do about them. The pause facilitates peacefulness and problem solving.

You learn to be less judgmental toward yourself and others. It encourages patience and teaches you how to objectively view events and emotions, through a more accepting filter.

You learn to use breathing to reduce anxiety and reduce reactionary behavior. The more you practice focused, slow breathing, the easier it becomes to tamp down anxiety, and gift yourself time to process events and emotions before you react.

You feel more satisfied in your job. When you can view workplace stressors with a more calming and proactive approach, it helps you feel empowered to positively address situations, leading to more job satisfaction.

Which of the previous benefits do you need to foster the most?

_____

_____

_____

_____

_____

_____

_____

_____

_____

_____

Why do you think you are having these issues? Be specific.

_____

_____

_____

_____

_____

_____

_____

_____

_____

_____

_____

It Bolsters Appreciation

Mindfulness not only helps you accept yourself just as you are, it also helps you be more open to listening to and learning from others, allowing you to see and appreciate your coworkers. It does this by reducing activity in the part of your brain that generates the story of your self—sometimes called the narrative self—and bringing your attention back to the present. Giving too much attention to you and your own story narrows your focus and prevents you from seeing or feeling when coworkers are being helpful. Use mindfulness to widen your attention so you can see and appreciate how coworkers often contribute to your ability to do your best work.

VIEW STRESS AS HELPFUL

In a study of 30,000 people, researchers at the University of Wisconsin-Madison found that people experiencing high levels of stress, who viewed their stress in a positive light (as something that energized them for any challenges), had lower mortality rates; those who believed their stress was only hurting them had the highest chance of dying. There's some evidence, as well, that suggests seeing the positive benefits stress can bring also keeps your blood vessels from constricting.

Mindfulness meditation can help you flip from thinking of stress as "all bad" to viewing stress as an energizing force that primes your body and brain for challenges. The next time you feel stress at work, pause to mindfully focus your attention on how your body is responding (increased heart rate, faster or more shallow breathing, sweaty palms); then tell yourself that these reactions are simply your body preparing you to rise to the challenge.

It may lessen stress if you can feel grateful that your faster heart rate is pumping oxygen throughout your body, sharpening your senses, and energizing your brain. If you can learn to view whatever is causing you to feel stressed as a *positive challenge* and recognize that any stress you feel is your body preparing to meet it, you may live longer.

Are there occasions when you feel stressed at work that you could now view as your body energizing your brain and preparing you to focus?

PART III

Heighten Your Intellectual Wellness

Intellectual wellness at work refers to your ability to engage in various activities to promote learning, critical thinking, and creative thinking in the workplace. If your intellectual abilities are being overestimated, underutilized, or taken for granted, you need strategies you can institute to bolster your intellectual wellness. In this section, we'll discuss the need to thrive at work, identify anything that is holding your intellectual needs hostage, offer strategies for bolstering intellectual stimulation and fulfillment, help you adjust your mindset, and offer ways to improve self-efficacy, all of which will advance your intellectual fulfillment at work.

> **"The comfort zone is a behavioral state within which a person operates in an anxiety-neutral condition, using a limited set of behaviors to deliver a steady level of performance, usually without a sense of risk."**
>
> —Alasdair White, musician

To know whether a lack of intellectual wellness is a problem for you, here's a simple either/or quiz to help you know where to begin. If you aren't either of the extremes, highlight or circle the one that is closest to the truth.

What's Your Mental Status at Work?

Engaged	or	Checked out
Confident	or	Stressed
Focused	or	Distracted
Motivated	or	Unfulfilled
Flourishing	or	Languishing
Energetic	or	Exhausted
Challenged	or	Bored
Overloaded	or	Underutilized
Valued	or	Invisible
Happy	or	Miserable

Which of your circled feelings from the previous page are most problematic and need to be addressed?

_____

_____

_____

_____

_____

_____

_____

_____

Write about why you're feeling this way, identifying the underlying causes and brainstorming ideas for improvement.

_____

_____

_____

_____

_____

_____

_____

_____

_____

For the quiz choices where you fit somewhere in the middle, describe where you are and why.

_____

_____

_____

_____

_____

_____

_____

_____

What can you do to move the needle in the desired direction?

_____

_____

_____

_____

_____

_____

_____

_____

_____

_____

_____

CHAPTER 6

Strive to Thrive

In work, thriving is about using your unique skills, being productive, achieving an elevated level of performance, and receiving financial reward. But to enjoy workplace wellness, it's also imperative that you feel a sense of fulfillment and enjoyment in your work. To thrive, you need to feel supported, encouraged, appreciated, and rewarded, but also intellectually challenged, happy, and fulfilled. When thriving, you experience vitality and feel a sense of progress or forward movement in your self-development.

Check the boxes below for each statement that applies to your workplace, then answer the questions on the next page.

☐ My creative and critical thinking is highly valued.

☐ My initiative and leadership skills are appreciated and encouraged.

☐ My curiosity, innovative approaches, and ideas are welcomed and fostered.

☐ I enjoy a cooperative, collaborative, supportive culture.

☐ I am utilizing my education, knowledge, experience, and talents.

☐ I am growing both personally and professionally.

☐ Resources for developing additional skills are provided.

☐ I am encouraged to learn and grow.

☐ My personal values are supported.

☐ I am treated fairly and feel supported by my coworkers.

☐ I feel valued and well rewarded.

☐ I am treated with respect.

☐ I feel like I belong.

☐ I feel a sense of fulfillment.

Which of the statements that don't apply are most important to your workplace wellness?

_____

_____

_____

_____

_____

_____

_____

Do you foresee any way to make what you need a reality in your current job situation?

_____

_____

_____

_____

_____

_____

_____

IDENTIFY ROADBLOCKS TO YOUR INTELLECTUAL WELL-BEING

Even if you've checked "Does Not Apply" only once on the previous list, that means there's still some room for improvement. Let's take a deep dive into why you're *not* thriving at work. The following questions are designed to provide insight into whatever roadblocks are in the way of your workplace wellness.

Are you happy at work? If not, why not?

_____

_____

_____

_____

_____

_____

_____

_____

_____

What about your workplace is problematic?

_____

_____

_____

_____

_____

_____

What positive or negative feelings do you have about your organization?

_____

_____

_____

_____

_____

_____

_____

_____

What positive or negative feelings do have about your manager?

_____

_____

_____

_____

_____

_____

_____

_____

_____

_____

What positive or negative feelings do you have about your coworkers?

_____

_____

_____

_____

_____

_____

Are you motivated by an intrinsic interest in your work? If no, why not?

_____

_____

_____

_____

_____

_____

Are your responsibilities intellectually stimulating? If no, why not?

_____

_____

_____

_____

_____

_____

Do you feel valued and respected? How does it manifest?

_____

_____

_____

_____

_____

_____

_____

_____

Four Ways to Know You're Thriving at Work

Navalent, a business consulting service, studied more than two hundred organizations and found that thriving at work requires success in four areas: professional (or intellectual), emotional, relational, and significance. They say you'll know you're thriving when:

- **You're developing** (professional thriving): You're regularly expanding your influence and capabilities.
- **You're confident** (emotional thriving): You feel emotionally safe, confident, and comfortable.
- **You're known** (relational thriving): You feel like, and are seen as, an essential part of a supportive community.
- **You're valued** (significance thriving): You feel significant and know your specific contributions are noticed and matter.

If you're not thriving in the four areas above, it's time to make changes.

Are you growing or stagnant? Where would you like to be in one year? Five years?

_____

_____

_____

_____

_____

_____

_____

Is what you do each day in alignment with your long-term goals?

_____

_____

_____

_____

_____

_____

_____

_____

_____

Is your job in alignment with your principles?

What kind of work—or work situation—would be more fulfilling?

FOCUS ON WHAT YOU CAN DO, ONE TASK AT A TIME

It seems all workplaces these days are *hyper*-focused on productivity and thus place enormous pressure on employees to do as much as they can, as fast as they can. Thriving at work does not mean being all things to all people, or being able to multitask like a champ and work miracles. Not only would trying to do so be detrimental to your intellectual wellness, but it's a simple truth that the only way to maintain sanity in an overwhelming workplace—and to have any concrete effect on that workplace—is to accept the reality of your limitations.

No matter how brilliant or hardworking, all humans have limitations. Your brain has massive capability to think, learn, grow, and do what you need it to do but, in truth, your brain functions best when it focuses on one task at a time. Multitasking has been repeatedly shown to reduce your capacity to do your best, most efficient work.

Instead of multitasking, try time-blocking, in which you block out tasks and complete them in order of priority, one at a time. Basically, you create a daily to-do list of essential, ongoing tasks. Then, order them from most important to least important and decide how much time you need to do each. Finally, create a timetable to structure your workday.

Time block your next few days. We'll start with an example here. Begin by creating a to-do list of the next five tasks (or projects) you need to accomplish. Order them in terms of priority.

1. _____

2. _____

3. _____

4. _____

5. _____

Now, break down the five tasks into three to five smaller, doable aspects that will allow you to accomplish the larger task; indicate how long you estimate each smaller task will take.

1. _____
  a. _____
  b. _____
  c. _____
  d. _____
  e. _____

2. _____
  a. _____
  b. _____
  c. _____
  d. _____
  e. _____

3. _____
  a. _____
  b. _____
  c. _____
  d. _____
  e. _____

4 _____
  a. _____
  b. _____
  c. _____
  d. _____
  e. _____

5. _____
  a. _____
  b. _____
  c. _____
  d. _____
  e. _____

> **"The 'secret' of those people who 'do so many things' and apparently so many difficult things, is that they do only one at a time."**
>
> —Peter F. Drucker,
> *The Effective Executive*

Now, choose which of the smaller tasks you will tackle *tomorrow*, order at least five of them in terms of priority, and estimate the time you'll need for each. Use this as your guide for time blocking your next day at work. Be sure to pat yourself on the back for every task you complete. Use this format to continue time blocking your workdays.

APPROX. TIME

1. _____ _____

2. _____ _____

3. _____ _____

4. _____ _____

5. _____ _____

Use an Hourglass to Focus

Celeste Headlee, author of *Do Nothing: How to Break Away from Overworking, Overdoing, and Underliving*, uses a thirty- or sixty-minute hourglass to improve focus and keep her on track. She simply turns it over when she begins a task, then, if her mind wanders, she glances at the hourglass to remind her that just a few minutes have passed since she began the task, which helps her quickly refocus on the project at hand.

> "Multitasking creates a dopamine addiction feedback loop, effectively rewarding the brain for losing focus and for constantly searching for external stimulation."

—Daniel J. Levitin, *The Organized Mind*

CHAPTER 7

Strategies to Improve Intellectual Wellness

Once you've identified what you need to thrive in your workplace, it's time to focus on specific strategies for manifesting your desired goals. You not only need to recognize what tactics you can employ to improve your intellectual wellness; you also need to adjust your mindset, improve your self-efficacy (competence and confidence), welcome feedback, bolster positivity, find your passion, recognize your accomplishments, and both feel and express gratitude. We'll cover all those topics going forward, setting you on the path to intellectual stimulation and fulfillment.

First, clearly define the steps you can take toward fulfilling your intellectual requirements at work. Here's a list of strategies you could adopt to improve your intellectual wellness while on the job:

1. Create long-term goals.
2. Document your successes.
3. Let your boss know what you want.
4. Ask for new responsibilities or training.
5. Volunteer to work on teams.
6. Find a professional mentor.
7. Create a career progress chart/timeline.
8. Map out *your* path to advancement.
9. Honor your principles.

Which strategies can you put into motion immediately?

_____

_____

_____

_____

_____

_____

Which strategies can you put into motion over time?

_____

_____

_____

_____

_____

What else could you do, specific to your situation?

_____

_____

_____

_____

_____

_____

What does steady growth look like?

_____

_____

_____

_____

_____

_____

_____

_____

_____

Where do you want to be in three years? Five years? What do you need to do to get there?

_____

_____

_____

_____

_____

_____

_____

_____

_____

_____

ADJUST YOUR MINDSET

According to Dr. Carol S. Dweck, author of *Mindset: The New Psychology of Success*, people typically have either a fixed mindset or a growth mindset. When you have a fixed mindset, you see your basic qualities, such as intelligence and talents, as fixed traits. Instead of making an effort to develop your attributes, you tend to *hope* that they're good enough to get where you want to go.

When you have a growth mindset, however, you believe that you can improve your intelligence and talents with effort. You see your attributes as the starting point, are very open to learning, and are more resilient.

To move from a fixed mindset to a growth mindset, use the following mindful technique:

- **Examine your thought process**. When challenged, be mindful of your thoughts. Are they conveying doubt about your abilities? Are they urging you to decline opportunities or rebuff feedback? Are they causing you to feel anxious or angry?

- **Pause to make a different choice.** Mindfully bring your focus to the present and *choose* to reject your fixed mindset. *Choose* to think and react positively to challenges and you will soon see options you typically may not have seen.

- **Question your fixed mindset attitudes.** If the fixed mindset communicates that you're not up to the task, reassure yourself that it's not true and politely inform your mindset that all successful people fail before they succeed. In other words, counter the negative fixed thoughts with statements that reflect a more open and expansive approach.

- **Take on the challenge.** A growth mindset teaches you to welcome expansion and eagerly take on new challenges, even when you're not fully confident that you'll succeed. You now recognize that growth itself is the reward you seek.

Over time, with diligent practice, you will transition from a fixed mindset to a growth mindset. When you operate from a growth mindset, you'll see what used to feel like negative feedback as a means for you to discover something new; you'll also learn to enjoy taking on new responsibilities and welcome challenges as opportunities for inner growth. Because your growth mindset will help you be more flexible and eager to take on challenges, you will soon be receiving positive feedback, succeeding regularly, and learning new things about yourself and others. More opportunities and more successful outcomes will follow.

> **"People's beliefs about their abilities have a profound effect on those abilities. Ability is not a fixed property; there is a huge variability in how you perform. People who have a sense of self-efficacy bounce back from failures; they approach things in terms of how to handle them rather than worrying about what can go wrong."**
>
> —Dr. Daniel Goleman, *Emotional Intelligence*

Do you have a fixed mindset? How does it hold you back?

_____

_____

_____

_____

_____

_____

What are the specific fixed thoughts that lead to anxiety or stress?

_____

_____

_____

_____

_____

What are the specific fixed thoughts that lead you to decline challenges?

_____

_____

_____

_____

_____

_____

Use this space to write statements that challenge or counter each of your fixed thoughts.

_____

_____

_____

_____

_____

_____

What would a growth mindset look like for you? How would it manifest?

_____

_____

_____

_____

_____

_____

"If you have the guts to keep making mistakes, your wisdom and intelligence leap forward with huge momentum."

—Holly Near, singer and songwriter

"**People who regard themselves as highly efficacious act, think, and feel differently from those who perceive themselves as inefficacious. They produce their own future, rather than simply foretell it.**"

—Dr. Albert Bandura,
Social Foundations of Thought and Actions

BOLSTER YOUR SELF-EFFICACY

Dr. Albert Bandura developed the cognitive theory known as self-efficacy, which he defines as having a locus of control over your ability to reach a specific goal. If *you* believe that you can succeed at a particular task, that self-generated and self-sustained confidence will motivate you to be proactive, and thereby help you succeed.

Workers who don't have strong self-efficacy are more likely to underestimate their abilities, shy away from challenges, and fear the worst—leaving them feeling overwhelmed, stressed, and eventually, depressed. Because they are confident, self-aware, and self-assured, someone with strong self-efficacy will inevitably be happier and healthier in the workplace, as evidenced in the comparison below:

High self-efficacy characteristics	Low self-efficacy characteristics
High self-esteem	Low self-esteem
Objectively sees and evaluates self	Focuses on failures
Willing to take risks; pivot to something new	Avoids taking risks or trying something new
Takes on tough or challenging problems	Hyper-focused on negative outcomes
Highly motivated and resilient	Feels overwhelmed
Has a clarity of purpose	Aversion to connection
Upbeat and optimistic	Susceptible to depression

Review the above lists and circle or highlight whatever applies to your current work situation.

Create a list of all the characteristics you'd like to jettison from your work persona.

_____

_____

_____

_____

_____

_____

_____

_____

Create a list of the characteristics you'd like to develop at work.

_____

_____

_____

_____

_____

_____

_____

_____

_____

_____

_____

Brainstorm ways to dump the negative and bolster the positive characteristics.

_____

_____

_____

_____

_____

_____

Think back to the last time you felt insecure at work and write something that counteracts this self-doubt.

_____

_____

_____

_____

_____

_____

_____

_____

"An intelligent person is never afraid or ashamed to find errors in his understanding of things."

—Bryant H. McGill, author

Think back to a time when you doubted your own abilities, but a coworker disagreed with your assessment and challenged those negative thoughts. How did this make you feel?

Recall a time you overcame a challenge. What did you learn about your capabilities from the experience?

When you feel strong and capable at work, what qualities or beliefs are driving that feeling?

_____

_____

_____

_____

_____

_____

Reflect on three to five times when you used your talents or skills to achieve something and describe how it felt to experience success.

_____

_____

_____

_____

"The lower the sense of self-efficacy, the higher the perceived burnout. If you find yourself on the wheel of weariness, you will be weakening your personal pulse and setting yourself up to be more susceptible to lowered self-efficacy."

—Dr. Jacinta M. Jiménez, *The Burnout Fix*

What are three things you appreciate most about yourself and why?

1. _____

2. _____

3. _____

What do others think are your best qualities and do you agree? Are these qualities being used to your advantage at work?

_____

_____

_____

_____

_____

_____

_____

_____

_____

_____

_____

_____

_____

_____

_____

How to Benefit from Feedback

Feedback is essential to progress, particularly when it's honest, accurate, productive, and inspires growth. If you want feedback that will help you improve your self-efficacy, move closer to your goals and grow, abide by the following four rules:

1. Only ask for feedback from people you admire, who know more about the subject than you do.

2. Ignore criticism from people you don't know or who don't know more than you.

3. Make the feedback giver feel honored in offering advice and give credence to anyone who helps you.

4. Always strive for specific feedback by asking the following questions:

   - *Can you specify what you like the least?* Asking for specifics avoids generic answers. You want to know exactly where you've gone wrong.

   - *Can you specify the aspects you like the best?* You want to know precisely what you're doing right, so you can expand in that direction.

   - *Specifically, why do you like it?* If they can't explain why they think it's good, ignore whatever they say.

If you still find it hard to seek or endure feedback, keep in mind that in the absence of feedback, it's hard to grow beyond where you are right now.

"Your assumptions are your windows on the world. Scrub them off every once in a while, or the light won't come in."

—Alan Alda, actor

FOSTER POSITIVITY AT WORK

According to the *Harvard Business Review*, a central driver of creative, productive performance is the mix of emotions, motivations, and perceptions a worker feels. When positive, they boost productivity—and workplace wellness! When negative, they detract.

Plus, once accentuating the positive and diminishing the negative becomes a mindset and habit you employ, you'll soon notice and appreciate how your work—and even simply being in your workplace—often contributes to, rather than detracts from, your overall wellbeing. Writing down your *positive* observations sets you on the path to noticing the positives more often.

Write five positive statements about your job, your work environment, or your coworkers.

1. _____

2. _____

3. _____

4. _____

5. _____

Do this every day for three months, and positivity will become a beneficial habit, guaranteed to improve your attitude, and make being at work a more pleasant experience.

Read Positive Content

Between the news and our social media feeds, it's easy to feel bombarded with negative messages. To bolster positivity, make a conscious choice to weed out or ignore anything negative. Instead, focus on reading only positive stories. You'll soon notice your mindset and intellectual well-being transform. It can be as easy as switching off the news when events feel overwhelming.

Notice Small Victories

To bolster your ability to offer yourself compassion and thereby strengthen your self-efficacy, focus on what you do well. Keep a journal in which you record any small victories at work when they occur and take time to compliment yourself on the page. The more you recognize your self-efficacy, the stronger it will grow.

FIND WAYS TO STAY THE COURSE

Just like any action plan, making changes at work requires ongoing discipline. Ideally, any efforts to improve your workplace wellness should include:

- **Motivation**: Multiple ways to bolster healthy behaviors.
- **Education**: Knowing the why and how of healthy choices.
- **Support**: Friends, family, and coworkers who encourage each other.
- **Accountability**: A way to track and reward progress.

How will you motivate yourself to improve your workplace wellness?

_____

_____

_____

_____

_____

_____

_____

_____

What information do you need to bolster new habits? Where can you find it?

_____

_____

_____

_____

_____

_____

_____

_____

_____

_____

_____

_____

Who will be your support system?

_____

_____

_____

_____

_____

_____

How will you hold yourself accountable?

_____

_____

_____

_____

_____

_____

_____

_____

_____

_____

_____

_____

Reward Yourself Often

Research has shown that rewarding yourself for any task you need to do (especially when it's something you don't particularly like to do or tend to resist doing), will *train your brain* to associate the task with pleasure. It doesn't matter how you reward yourself, as long as you do it *immediately* after completing the task and whatever you do brings *genuine* pleasure. Best to steer clear of food or alcohol pleasures, but a bubble bath, a walk in nature, calling a friend, watching your favorite sitcom, or canoodling with your beloved are all good ways to link pleasure to whatever task you want to do more often.

RECOGNIZE AND RECORD YOUR GRATITUDE

In multiple studies, feeling and expressing gratitude has been shown to increase happiness. Here's how you can use gratitude to feel better about work:

1. Choose a specific time each day to practice gratitude.

2. Decide how you want to express your gratitude. You can write in a gratitude journal, slip pieces of paper into a gratitude jar, use the "notes" function on your phone, or even use a gratitude app (see below).

3. Focus on the good things or positive interactions that happened at work, then simply write down what they were and include a statement of gratitude: to others, to yourself, or to the universe, if you like.

4. You can also express gratitude for how negative situations were resolved. Consider challenges you faced during the day and find something positive within them. This will help shift your perspective and express gratitude for what is working.

Try a Gratitude App

If it helps you make time to express your gratitude, using apps is fine. Here are a few you can find online:

- Gratitude-Journal Prompts *(www.gratefulness.me)*
- Three Lines Gratitude Journal or Three Lines Diary (via *play.google.com*)
- Reflectly *(reflectly.app)*
- 365 Gratitude Journal *(365gratitudejournal.com)*
- Happy Feed *(happyfeed.co)*
- Whole *(getwhole.co)*

RECOGNIZE YOUR CONTRIBUTIONS

Employees are happiest when they feel that they are contributing value to something or someone important to them. It could be as simple as making a high-quality product that will prove useful to many, or providing a crucial service to a community. It could be supporting fellow employees, or boosting your company's profits. As long as the rewards are *meaningful* to you, and it's clear how your contribution is important, you will be happier and more productive at work.

What contributions does your work make to society?

_____

_____

_____

_____

_____

_____

_____

_____

_____

_____

_____

_____

_____

_____

Are these contributions sufficient to keep you happy at work? If not, why not?

_____

_____

_____

_____

Are you where you want to be? If not, what kind of work would be more fulfilling for you, in terms of valuable contributions to society?

_____

_____

_____

_____

"A part of me was like, 'Man, do I even like doing this anymore?' That whole thing of 'I'm in my thirties, and I sing and write songs while people are fighting wars in Iraq.' You know? So, everything had to have more meaning, and it couldn't just be about making money. So, I took a minute."

—Maxwell, singer and songwriter

"Follow your passion; it will lead you to your purpose."

—Oprah Winfrey, television producer and author

FIND YOUR PASSION

Those who have a passion for what they do as work are often far happier than those who don't. Of course, it's not always easy to make that happen, but if you don't even know what you are passionate about, it's impossible to align your passion with what you do for a living. To help you figure out what makes you so happy that you achieve the thrill of flow when working, answer the following questions.

What were five of the most deeply immersive moments you had at work last year? Where were you and what were you doing?

1. _____
2. _____
3. _____
4. _____
5. _____

Do those moments have anything in common? Maybe they all took place outdoors or involved other people. Is there a common denominator that contributes to your job satisfaction?

_____

_____

_____

_____

_____

Your past interests and hobbies can also provide clues. What do you love to do when you have free time? What did you love to do when you were younger? Are you using any of those skills in your current job?

_____

_____

_____

_____

_____

"If you haven't found [your passion] yet, keep looking. Don't settle. As with all matters of the heart, you'll know when you find it."

—Steve Jobs, cofounder of Apple Inc.

> **"I love making money, but you can't live your life waiting to get rich in a job that no longer feeds you artistically."**
>
> —Julianna Margulies, actor

If you could go back to school or seek training to embark on a new career, what would you choose to study? What would excite you?

_____

_____

_____

_____

_____

_____

Once you've identified what lights you up, or has the potential to, block out fifteen minutes today to try it and then write about how it made you feel.

_____

_____

_____

_____

_____

Then, at least once a week, use your new pursuit to stave off burnout and keep your energy levels humming.

PART IV

Advance Your Financial Wellness

While it's true that most of us need to work to earn a living, it's also true that few of us would do our jobs if we weren't being paid to do them. Money is a strong motivator. No matter where you fall on the salary scale, whether entry level or CEO, feeling *fairly* compensated and learning how to grow your wealth are both important to workplace wellness.

Employees under monetary stress are less likely to engage with the company culture, are less social, and may unconsciously allow resentment to justify slacking off. Or, it might even lead them to jamming up the works, inadvertently creating problems for other employees. Bad moods and discontent can be infectious.

Aside from its impact on overall health, being fairly compensated can also affect how productive you are at work. When you feel more financially secure, it helps you focus on your tasks rather than worry about money. Financial wellness provides the confidence and assurance you need to tackle work pressures.

"You either master money, or, on some level, money masters you."

—Tony Robbins, author, coach, and speaker

Basics of Financial Wellness

It's not as complicated as you might think. To maintain basic financial wellness, you need to make sure you:

- Control your day-to-day and month-to-month expenses.
- Keep any spending well within your means (that is, avoid living off credit).
- Make sure you're financially prepared for emergencies.
- Utilize information and tools necessary to make good financial decisions.
- Have a short- and long-term plan to meet financial goals.
- Create sufficient financial freedom to enjoy life.

To achieve financial wellness, make sure you're taking advantage of all available benefits, contributing to a retirement fund, and are aware of and focused upon potential financial growth.

CHAPTER 8
Take a Financial Assessment

Financial wellness goes beyond asking for a raise. When you have a comprehensive understanding of your finances, you can create effective strategies for dividing—potentially automatically—your paychecks to cover bills, savings, investments, and other commitments. Financial wellness means that you are successfully meeting your short-term needs, while also working toward your long-range goals.

To promptly address your financial wellness, answer the following questions:

Does your financial compensation feel fair, or just adequate?

_____

How much do you reasonably need to make so you can live a balanced, healthy life?

_____

Are you saving money? Making investments? Building capital?

_____

How much higher does your compensation need to go for you to feel secure and happy in your job?

_____

Do you have benefits that make it all worthwhile? Are you taking full advantage of your benefits?

Do you have adequate health insurance? Other insurances?

Do you have an adequate emergency fund (at least three to six months' worth of expenses)?

Have you ever had a frank conversation with your employer about your financial recompense?

_____

Are there sufficient opportunities for advancement?

_____

Is there competition for higher-level jobs? How can you overcome this?

_____

Do you have a plan for moving up in the company? Is your boss aware of your desire for advancement?

_____

What do you need to do to advance? Do you need additional skills? If so, what are they?

_____

What would be a reasonable time frame for moving to the next level?

_____

If you're underpaid, outline any specific contributions you bring to the bottom line, then ask for the raise you deserve. Also, if you have any issues at home, such as impulsive buying, not keeping track of expenses (see page 182), or failing to accumulate savings, make a concerted effort to change your habits and improve your financial savviness.

Financial Insecurity Is Real

A Mental Health America survey on workplace health of more than five thousand employees across seventeen industries in the United States found:

- employees do not feel financially secure until they earn at least $60,000 to $80,000 per year;
- nearly 80 percent of respondents reported earning an annual individual income of less than $80,000, with 65 percent of those respondents earning less than $60,000;
- among the lower earners, 58 percent reported that they worry about not having enough money to pay for their living expenses;
- nearly 34 percent could not afford healthcare;
- two in three employees could not save for an emergency;
- respondents felt they needed at least $80,000 per year in income to enable them to save for emergencies.

EXPENSE TRACKER

INCOME	AMOUNT
Income 1	
Income 2	
Income 3	
Total	

HOUSING	AMOUNT
Mortgage/rent	
Phone	
Electricity	
Gas/oil	
Water/sewer	
Waste removal	
Internet/cable	
Maintenance/repairs	
Supplies	
Other	
Subtotal	

ENTERTAINMENT	AMOUNT
Streaming services/movie rentals	
Music downloads/other purchases	
Movies	
Concerts	
Sporting events	
Theater	
Other event admission	
Other	
Subtotal	

INSURANCE	AMOUNT
Home	
Medical/dental/vision	
Life	
Other	
Subtotal	

TRANSPORTATION	AMOUNT
Vehicle payment	
Bus/taxi/rideshare fare	
Licensing/inspection fee	
Fuel	
Maintenance	
Car wash	
Other	
Subtotal	

CHILD(REN)	AMOUNT
Childcare	
Medical/dental	
Toys/games	
Activities	
Clothing/gear	
Allowance	
Other	
Subtotal	

FOOD	AMOUNT
Groceries	
Dining out	
Coffee/drinks	
Other	
Subtotal	

PERSONAL CARE	AMOUNT
Medical/dental	
Hair/nails/massages	
Clothing	
Dry cleaning	
Gym membership/classes	
Organization dues/fees	
Other	
Subtotal	

LOANS	AMOUNT
Personal	
Student	
Credit card	
Credit card	
Credit card	
Credit card	
Other	
Subtotal	

SAVINGS OR INVESTMENTS	AMOUNT
Retirement account	
Investment account	
Savings account	
Other	
Subtotal	

LEGAL	AMOUNT
Attorney	
Alimony	
Other	
Subtotal	

PETS	AMOUNT
Food	
Vet	
Insurance	
Toys	
Grooming	
Boarding/daycare	
Other	
Subtotal	

TAXES	AMOUNT
Federal	
State	
Local	
Other	
Subtotal	

GIFTS AND DONATIONS	AMOUNT
Charity	
Gift	
Donation	
Other	
Subtotal	

TOTAL INCOME	
TOTAL EXPENSES	
DIFFERENCE (income minus expenses)	

MONTHLY BUDGET

MONTHLY INCOME	
SOURCE	AMOUNT
Total	

MONTHLY EXPENSES	
SOURCE	AMOUNT
Total	

DAILY EXPENSES	MONTHLY SAVINGS

MONTHLY INCOME	
SOURCE	AMOUNT
Total	

MONTHLY EXPENSES	
SOURCE	AMOUNT
Total	

DAILY EXPENSES

MONTHLY SAVINGS

ASK FOR HELP

After many of his employees came to him for financial advice, the founder of Pacific Market Research, Andrew Rosenkranz, created employee-centric financial counseling and money management programs. One of the most lasting outcomes was positive peer pressure at work.

Employees formed teams of two to four people to continue encouraging each other to adopt and adhere to solid financial principles. Virtually all the participants in the program said they would recommend the supportive culture to a friend or coworker, with eight out of ten saying they would do so strongly. The same number (78 percent) reported that they made positive changes in their spending habits. For Pacific Market Research, the training boosted employee perceptions that their employer cares about their well-being (increasing from 48 percent to 81 percent).

The journey to financial wellness begins with financial literacy. A financially literate employee is schooled on:

- The true worth of their benefits;
- How to maximize benefits;
- How to set and manage financial goals;
- How to manage debt;
- Retirement planning;
- Emergency relief.

Have you asked your supervisor or human resources for financial education? If you have or if you do, what topics would be most helpful? Budgeting? Investing? Income progression? Credit management?

_____

_____

_____

_____

_____

_____

_____

_____

Who among your fellow employees would be most likely to support you in this quest?

_____

_____

_____

_____

_____

_____

_____

_____

_____

_____

Afterword: Before You Quit

Certainly, all aspects of your workplace contribute to your wellness on the job. Any serious or unsolvable imbalance in any one of the factors we've discussed—physical, emotional, intellectual, or financial wellness—may well cause you to consider whether your current job is the right one for you. However, changing jobs offers no guarantee that you'll land in a superior place, and making a concerted effort to effect whatever changes are possible in your current circumstances is a marvelous way to know yourself better, assert yourself, and grow. Thus, before you start planning your departure, make sure that you have first tried the following:

- Pinpointing and fully addressing the problems affecting your workplace wellness.

- Taking responsibility for all the changes you could make to improve your situation.

- Changing your behavior or routine, improving your emotional regulation, better managing your anxiety by, for example, trying meditation and mindfulness.

- Setting boundaries that make your workplace a safe and rewarding place to be.

- Taking on new challenges, bolstering your self-efficacy, finding a mentor, or adjusting your attitude.

- Finding contentment outside of work, or a way to value your (and/or your company's) contributions enough to make staying a positive.

If you've done *all of the above* (plus all the remaining suggestions offered in this book) and are still unhappy in your current work situation, it may well be time to seek a new opportunity.

WHEN YOU CHANGE JOBS

If you're going to change jobs, look for a company that recognizes the importance of and practices workplace wellness. If they do, it tends to be reflected in their core image and messaging. Study their website to discover if the company:

- promotes itself as putting its people first and rewarding their contributions;
- communicates the importance of building a healthy, strong workforce through its brand message and marketing efforts;
- actively supports inclusivity, equality, and nondiscrimination;
- makes employees feel like they're a part of a family; and
- makes wellness a priority.

If you do your homework, you'll avoid jumping from a frying pan into a fire.

Now that our journey is complete, we hope you've learned useful skills and feel inspired to make changes that will improve your workplace wellness. Because you spend so much time at work, your work environment needs to be supportive, encouraging, beneficial, and, above all, safe.

About the Author

Susan Reynolds has written, co-authored, or edited more than 25 nonfiction books, primarily self-help works on everything from finance to meditation to neuroscience. Her books include *Finding Your Authentic Self, 5-Minute Productivity Workbook, Fire Up Your Writing Brain*, and *Train Your Brain to Get Happy*. She writes blogs for Psychologytoday.com and on fireupyourwritingbrain.com.